ARISTOPHANES

Oxford University Press, Amen House, London E.C.4

GLASGOW   NEW YORK   TORONTO   MELBOURNE   WELLINGTON
BOMBAY   CALCUTTA   MADRAS   KARACHI   LAHORE   DACCA
CAPE TOWN   SALISBURY   NAIROBI   IBADAN   ACCRA
KUALA LUMPUR   HONG KONG

ARISTOPHANES

A STUDY

By

GILBERT MURRAY

Regius Professor of Greek in the
University of Oxford

OXFORD
AT THE CLARENDON PRESS

FIRST PUBLISHED 1933
REPRINTED LITHOGRAPHICALLY
IN GREAT BRITAIN
AT THE UNIVERSITY PRESS, OXFORD
FROM SHEETS OF THE FIRST EDITION
1965

TO MY OLD FRIEND

G. B. S.

LOVER OF IDEAS AND HATER OF CRUELTY

WHO HAS FILLED MANY LANDS WITH LAUGHTER

AND

WHOSE COURAGE HAS NEVER FAILED

PREFACE

THERE is little or no research in this book. If I have been moved to write it, the reason is that I have long felt dissatisfied both with the accounts of Aristophanes which seem to be generally accepted, and notably with the chapter upon him in my own *Ancient Greek Literature*—published in 1897. It is only late in life that I have learnt to care for Aristophanes and, I hope, to understand him.

In times like these one often longs for the return to earth of one of the great laughing philosophers of the past. In the War one longed for a breath of Voltaire to show the madness of men and the unhealthy superstitions in which they were nursed, or for Erasmus to induce them for a space to be gentle and honest with one another, and to think a moment or two before they struck or lied. But for many years I have wished quite particularly for Aristophanes, and wondered whether, like the great men who rise from the dead in two of his own comedies, he could bring us later generations some help. Could he fight against our European war-fevers and nationalisms as he fought against those of his own country, facing unpopularity—facing death, if it must be—yet always ready with his gallant laughter and never collapsing into spitefulness or mere self-pity? He might do it, if only the Fascisti and Nazis and Ogpus could refrain from killing him, and the British authorities from forbidding him to land in England. The world badly needs a man of genius who could make whole nations listen to him, and who would at the same time fight for the great causes that seem now so nearly lost, for generosity and kindliness between nations and classes, for poetry and high culture—and even for something which the ancients called Piety—in the individual life.

The misjudgements passed upon Aristophanes come, I should say, generally from three main causes. First, the man is so vividly alive that people cannot help using some current catchword or political term to describe him. They begin perhaps by calling him 'a Tory journalist' and comparing him to Canning in the *Anti-Jacobin*, and then they find that such a label only suits one facet of his character, and is false to a dozen others. For after all there were no Tories in ancient Athens, nor yet Whigs, nor even journalists. And if Aristophanes disliked the ascendancy of the mob as heartily as the *Morning Post*, he hated militarism and cruelty as much as the *Manchester Guardian*, and he exposed the absurdity of the world's solemn façades as vividly as a 'Low' cartoon. But the plain fact is, of course, that he does not fit any of our present-day pigeon-holes and has to be considered by himself, as a new specimen.

Again, critics who are startled or repelled by the frequent indecency of his language, so contrary to the conventions of serious literature in

Greece, think of Aristophanes as coarse and boisterous, like some loud fellow in a public bar, who
may be funny but has no manners. I have tried
in my first chapter to explain why I think this
view mistaken and due mainly to a failure of historical, or perhaps anthropological, imagination.

Then there is the interesting, and perhaps
insoluble, question of τὸ γελοῖον—'laughter' or
'humour', in which Ancient Greece and modern
England sometimes seem to stand alone against
the rest of the world, much as they do in their
idealization of 'sportsmanship'. It is characteristic
of both that we do not think of laughter as
necessarily, or even usually, unkind. Aristotle lays
it down that one of the tests of a good joke is that
it must not cause pain to the object of it; and we in
England habitually laugh at the things we love
and respect far more than at those which we hate.
In many European countries, on the other hand,
if one may judge from the comic papers, laughter
is mostly meant to hurt—or at least, public laughter:
for it certainly is not so in private life. And consequently the majority of critics credit Aristophanes
with a grim and conscientious hatred of all the
things he laughs at—notably such objects as Euripides, Socrates, and women. My own view is that
we must distinguish, and that the distinction as a
rule is not difficult, for when Aristophanes does
hate a thing he takes some pains to let us know it.

A description is always made clearer by a contrast; and for the sake of such contrast as well as for

its own historical interest I have added a chapter on that other master of Greek Comedy, Menander, about whom our knowledge has so greatly increased since the publication of the Cairo papyrus in 1907.

Of course when I look again at the pages of those from whom I have learnt so much, of Kock and Meineke, of Blaydes, Van Leeuwen, and J. W. White, of Eduard Meyer and Croiset, of Rogers and many fine living scholars, I feel that in the points where I venture to differ from them I may well be wrong. I may have overstated my case, exaggerated certain parts of my subject and unduly suppressed others. I can only give my sincere impression of an author with whose works, as a background to Greek tragedy, I have long been familiar. I see him devoted to three great subjects, Peace, Poetry, and the philosophic criticism of life. He laughs, and cannot help laughing, about all of them, except indeed sometimes about the first; for the loss of Peace means ultimately the subjection of all life to the reign of brute force, and that, even to the Prince of Comedy, is too ghastly a thing for laughter.

I wish to express my thanks to two old pupils, Mr. F. W. Hall, President of St. John's, and Mr. J. D. Denniston, Fellow of Hertford, for their advice and criticism, and to Messrs. George Allen and Unwin, Ltd., for their permission to reprint several passages of verse translation.

CONTENTS

CHAPTER I

ANCIENT GREEK COMEDY: ARISTOPHANES' BACKGROUND

(*Daitalês, Babylonians, Acharnians*)

To understand the Old Attic Comedy it is necessary to make some effort of the historical, and indeed of the anthropological, imagination. The wit, the refinement, the high literary culture of comedy, and still more the rare public spirit and courage with which Aristophanes pled for reasonableness and peace throughout a fierce and dangerous period of war fever, are hard to reconcile with the indecency of language and sometimes of incident in most of the plays, or with the occasional foul-mouthed abuse of individuals. The traditional explanation is either to suggest simply that Aristophanes was a boisterous and rollicking blade whose high spirits habitually overcame him, or, rather more thoughtfully, to speak of 'that peculiar inebriety of mind which the Greeks showed in everything relating to Dionysus'.

'This festal jollity of comedy,' say Müller and Donaldson, 'at once broke through the restraints of decent behaviour and morality which, on other occasions, were strictly observed in those days. . . . The whole was regarded as the wild drollery of an ancient carnival. When the period of universal inebriety and licensed frolic had passed away all recollection of what had been seen and done was dismissed.'

This explanation certainly contains a grain of truth. All Comedy involves what modern psychologists call a Release, and this element of release is even more clear in ancient drama than in modern. After standing long at drill in tight uniforms, we like to undo our buttons and loll. After the habitual decorum of behaviour and respect for dignitaries which is imposed on us by the social conventions under which we live, we welcome in comedy an imaginative release from the proprieties. Release, and not latent cruelty, explains the pleasure with which an audience sees a film hero knocking respectable people into tubs of whitewash. Release, and not secret scepticism, is the motive of Aristophanes in flinging mockery at Dionysus and other gods,[1] and of medieval mummers at their Feasts of Fools, turning bishops and nuns and saints and even the communion chalice into ridicule.

Yet, important as it is, the element of release does not quite explain the obscenities of Aristophanes. A dramatic poem like the *Acharnians* or the *Frogs*, or even the *Lysistrata*, is not the extemporization of a drunken frolic, nor anything remotely like it. It is a work of art, written in exquisite style and full of pointed wit, with much shrewd and high-minded criticism of public affairs,

---

[1] Did the medieval comedians ever ridicule the Virgin? I do not think Attic Comedy was ever blasphemous against Athena. Of course the release is only relative.

as well as remarkable knowledge of the best literature. Revelling and reckless jollity, though *verae
causae*, do not explain the problem. Even the
things that specially strike us as indecent are not
generally like the blundering excesses of drunkenness.

Our ancient evidence gives the true explanation,
and our present anthropological knowledge enables
us to understand it. Aristotle tells us simply that
Comedy originated ἀπὸ τῶν ἐξαρχόντων τὰ φαλλικά,
'from the leaders of the phallic performances', and
vases as well as literary evidence show that the
actors in the Old Comedy regularly wore large
visible artificial phalli as part of their stage dress.[1]
It seems to us at first blush almost impossible to
imagine a highly intellectual piece like the *Frogs*,
or an exquisitely fanciful poem like the *Birds* performed in such outrageous costume. Yet there is
the fact and we have to understand it.

The first point to realize is that it is ritual, and
highly important ritual. No one who has read
Thucydides can forget the terrible effect produced
in Athens in 416 B.C. by what is called the mutilation of the Hermae; that is, the act of breaking or
knocking off the phalli of the figures of Hermes
which stood in front of public buildings and many
private houses. No one can misunderstand the

---

[1] Ar. *Poet.* ch. 4; Cornford, *Comedy*, pp. 20, 182; Pickard-Cam-
bridge, *Dithyramb*, &c., p. 237, n.; cf. *Wasps*, 1343, *Thesm.* 62,
239 (?), 643, 1114, *Pax*, 142, *Lys.* 863, 991, *Ach.* 158, 592, *Clouds*,
653.

profound seriousness of the Thesmophoria and other religious festivals in which artificial phalli were carried as offerings. To talk of indecency in this connexion is to apply altogether wrong standards. The most obvious and pressing desire of a primitive community was continued life; its chief fear was death or barrenness. And the ideas of fertility or barrenness were applied without differentiation to the fruits of the fields, the increase of flocks and herds, and the births of the tribe itself.[1] Fruitfulness was the object of the most ordinary prayers, the substance of the most usual blessings. The male organ of generation was taken by the majority of the Indo-European peoples, as well as by Semites and Egyptians, as the chief symbol of this continued life and fertility, the magic charm against the influences of barrenness and death. It is only recently that a discovery has been made which seems to afford a clue to these ideas. Anthropologists have shown that most very primitive peoples do not associate the bearing of children with sexual intercourse, but attribute it to all kinds of other causes.[2] One can only suppose that the discovery—for a great and strange discovery it was—that births of children were the result of a

[1] See Dieterich, *Mutter Erde*, chap. i.

[2] Frazer, *Totemism and Exogamy*, i. 189 ff., citing Spencer and Gillen, *Native Tribes*, p. 265, *Northern Tribes*, pp. 330 ff.; Hartland, *Primitive Paternity*, i. 254, ii. 250 ff.; Malinowsky, *Sexual Life of Savages*, pp. 181, 183 ff., 295; Vürtheim, *Aesch. Schutzflehende*, pp. 42 ff.

Gamos between the sexes, and did not occur without it, made at some early time an overwhelming impression on the mind of the Egyptians and other inhabitants of Eastern Mediterranean lands. It seemed as if the clue to fertility had at last been found. No longer need there be any fear of famine or cattle-plague or the dying out of the tribe. In the Egyptian religion and, according to Herodotus, in the Pelasgian or aboriginal religion of Greece, the phallus takes its part not merely in every agricultural and pastoral rite, but in most regions of religious worship.

Was the whole of such ritual of necessity licentious? Quite certainly not. No doubt it gave opportunity for licence, and the enjoyment of an obscene joke was presumably much the same in Aristophanes and his audience as in Shakespeare and his. But no one could apply the term 'licentious' to the stately and modest processions of the Thesmophoria or the Eleusinia; nay, in all probability most of the moral taboos and ideals of sexual purity which play such a considerable part in classical and Hellenistic ethics originated in these fertility cults and the anxiety to commit no error or offence which might interfere with their due fruitfulness. Anarchic lust was the offence of all others to be avoided. In the same way one may ask whether the worship of Dionysus of necessity led to drunkenness. The answer would be: on certain ritual occasions, yes; but certainly not to habitual or indiscriminate drunkenness. In an interesting inscription found near the Pnyx[1] which records the rules of a Dionysiac thiasos called 'The Iobacchoi' we find severe penalties attached to drunkenness or misbehaviour on the part of the votaries. It is not difficult to show the prevalence of a desire in classical times to make the phallic rites as decent and seemly as could be managed. The evidence is abundant and need not be detailed here. Yet, of course, it must be realized that such refinement is an aftergrowth. It comes with the growth of self-consciousness, and is really a step towards the abolition of the whole species of rite. In its origin intoxication was itself worshipped as a form of divine possession; the exaltation of the symbol of generation was in all likelihood actually intended to stimulate sexual desire and bring about the births of which it held the promise. In particular the Κῶμος or Revel of Dionysus implied a Γάμος or general union of the sexes, and without such a Gamos it would have failed of its purpose. That is why, under slight disguises, most of the extant plays of Aristophanes end with a Gamos;[2] it is also why, as late as Menander, the foundling child which plays such a large part in his plots, though no longer of divine birth, as it is in Euripides, is nearly always born as the result of a Dionysiac festival. The same ideas were present in the

---

[1] Dittenberger, *Sylloge* , ed. 2, 737.
[2] See Cornford, *Origin of Attic Comedy*, chap. 2.

May Day revels of the Middle Ages, and are doubtless responsible for the romantic and irregular births of most of the Arthurian knights.

To understand Aristophanic Comedy we must see it in its place in a chain of development. The first stage, long before Aristophanes, must have been a phallic Kômos intended to stimulate the fertility of the land, the flocks, and the people. About a hundred years after him we find the New Comedy, with no phallic dress, no indecency of language—at least in the hands of its greatest master, Menander—but only certain reminiscences of Dionysiac myths and a tendency, not yet extinct in comedy, to end with a romantic marriage. Aristophanic Comedy itself has the great ritual phalli, though it very seldom mentions them; it ends with a Gamos scene; and it has traces in its language of the ritual orgy on which it was based. Plots like that of the *Lysistrata*, in which the women strike in order to end the war, or the *Ecclesiazusae*, which ends in a communal Gamos of the sort proposed by Plato in the Fifth Book of the *Republic*, are not original efforts after obscenity for its own sake; they are methods by which the ancient ritual has been modified into Comedy. In other plays, such as the *Clouds, Frogs*, and *Birds*, the process has gone much farther: there is no trace of phallic ritual in the plot and practically none in the language.

There are three passages in which Aristophanes

gives an account of his own services to the art of
Comedy and the direction in which he has improved it.[1] These used to be a puzzle to commentators and were sometimes explained as being
simply ironical; but in the light of the above discussion they can be understood without difficulty.
He does not boast of his 'wild drollery' and
licence; he does not accuse his rivals of dullness
and prudery. Quite the reverse.

In the parabasis of the *Clouds*, second edition,
he refers to the ill success of the first (518 ff.):

> Spectators, I will tell you the plain truth. . . . Because
> I thought you a refined audience, and this the cleverest
> (σοφώτατ' ἔχειν) of my comedies, I gave you the first
> taste of the work that had cost me the greatest pains.
> And then I retired, beaten by vulgar fellows, in a way
> I did not deserve.

He speaks of the success of his earliest play, the
Daitalês, with its good young man and its bad
young man, and appeals to the audience who
admired that play to do justice to its sister,
the *Clouds*.

> See how modest (σώφρων) she is by nature. In the
> first place she does not bring on a great phallos of
> stitched leather to make the slaves (or 'boys') laugh;
> she does not mock at bald heads; she does not dance
> preposterous dances. The old man who says the lines
> does not go round hitting those present with a stick, to
> ·hide the badness of the jokes. She does not rush in with
> blazing torches, does not scream 'Whew, whew!', but

[1] *Clouds*, 518; *Pax*, 736; *Wasps*, 1015.

comes on trusting to herself and her verses. I am what I am; a poet who does not give himself airs. I do not try to cheat you by bringing on the same points twice and three times; I show my art by bringing forward ideas always new, none like the last and all clever.

He goes on to take credit for the way in which he had attacked Cleon at the height of his power and let him alone after his death or 'fall'.

In the parabasis of the *Peace* there is a similar passage (736 ff.). The Chorus claims high praise for Aristophanes from the theatre because

in the first place he, and he only, stopped the fashion of making jokes at ragged clothes, and fighting with lice; he was the first to despise and abolish those eternal dough-kneading Heracleses and hungry Heracleses; he put an end to the slaves who run away and deceive everybody and are beaten on purpose; the slaves they brought on weeping so that a fellow-slave might make jokes at their stripes. . . . He removed all that bad stuff, that lumber, those ignoble buffooneries, and made our art great, built it high like a tower with great verses and ideas and jests not of the market-place. He did not attack women or poor little private men, but, with a sort of Heracles temper, went straight for the greatest foe.[1]

The self-praise is of course humorous; in some points it is exaggerated, since he did not entirely abstain from all the 'ignoble buffooneries' that he mentions. There is some fun made out of a beating in the *Frogs*, there is a slave brought on weeping

[1] See below, p. 64 f..

in the *Knights*, there is a spirited fight not indeed
with lice, but with bugs, which are not essentially
more high-toned, in the *Clouds*; but in the main
the claim made here is true. True or not, however, the important point is that Aristophanes
made it. He did consider that he had found
Comedy indecent, coarse, common, and what is
called 'low-brow', and built it up into something
artistic, intellectual, public-spirited, and genuinely
brilliant. He made it σοφὸν καὶ Δεξιόν. He bids
the audience pack up his ideas in their chests till
next year, together with the usual citrons, and 'all
their garments will smell of Δεξιότης' (*Wasps*,
1056 ff.). He also claims to have made it modest
or respectable (σώφρων), or at least to have removed its more glaring indecencies. He never
made his Muse a procuress (*Wasps*, 1025 ff.) or
took bribes or blackmail from immoral characters
who were afraid of being attacked. He also claims
credit—very justly—for courage and public spirit,
but that is another question and will be considered
later.

The important thing is to see the Old Comedy
in its historical setting, to realize that the phallic
costume is not a gratuitous indecency put in for
indecency's sake, like certain things in Catullus
or Martial or, for that matter, in Shakespeare, but
a piece of tradition which once dominated the
whole performance, as it still does, for instance, in
the *Lysistrata*, and which for ritual and traditional

reasons could not easily be ignored, but which through the greater part of Aristophanes has not much more importance in itself or more influence on the rest of the drama than the wig of an Elizabethan actor had upon Hamlet, or the hideous deformities which he inherits from the medieval clown have on the wit of Mr. Punch.

The form of Attic Comedy has been the subject of much discussion. Hardly any one denies its origin ἀπὸ τῶν ἐξαρχόντων τὰ φαλλικά, but there has been a curious reluctance to admit the obvious conclusion that it is based on a religious rite, and was not a mere extempore piece of coarse buffoonery. There is enough evidence in the extant comedies of Aristophanes to enable us to see in general outline what sort of rite it was. In the centre was the *Parabasis*, a scene in which the Chorus comes forward and addresses the audience on behalf of the poet. The Parabasis has a very marked construction: introductory anapaests in praise, usually, of the poet, ending in a *Pnîgos* or long sentence to be pronounced in one breath; then an Odê or song and an Epirrhêma or speech about contemporary affairs, followed by an Antôdê and Antepirrhêma. What is even more curious, the Parabasis usually drops all pretence of dramatic illusion. At most, a chorus of Clouds may speak as Clouds, a chorus of Knights as Knights, but even then they do so without

deference to the plot or situation. In some plays
the Parabasis is repeated.

Whatever its origin, whether it is a survival of
the free comments of the Dionysiac Chorus upon
their neighbours and the Government, or an at-
tenuated remnant of an Agôn or Contest between
two Choruses—as in the *Lysistrata*—it seems clear
that the Parabasis is a nugget of unassimilated
ritual embedded in the structure of the play.

In the earlier part of the Comedy before the
Parabasis we have regularly a Prologue or Exposition, an entry of the Chorus, and an Agôn or
Contest. This contest is the essential scene; the
rest of the play hangs upon it. It is normally—
perhaps always except in the *Clouds*—a battle between the Hero and his Enemy, in which the Enemy
always begins the attack and is always defeated.

After the Parabasis comes a series of episodes
which until recently were considered to be subject
to no particular law of composition, but have been
made much more intelligible by Mr. Cornford's
analysis. He shows that most of the plays end
with a Kômos and Gamos, which is just what one
would expect. In many of them a female character
is introduced who has no relation to the plot of
the play except to make the Gamos possible. In
several cases she is actually anonymous. Before this
final Kômos-Gamos there are practically always
a sacrifice and a feast, with a string of unwelcome visitors who wish to share in the food and

are driven away. In some plays there is a suggestion of some resurrection or rebirth, and in several
a rejuvenation either of the Hero, who is normally
a witty Old Man, or some other Old Man, like
Demos in the *Knights*. In one at least of the lost
plays, the *Gêras*, there seems to have been a rejuvenation of the whole Chorus.

It is impossible not to see in these persistent
elements of structure the remains of those rites
connected with the renewal of the year or of the
life of the earth which are known to us in so many
parts of the world and have survived even in
northern Europe and in the English Mummers'
Play. We need not here inquire more closely
into the particular points of ritual involved. It is
enough to realize that Aristophanes in composing
his comedies was working in a traditional ritual
pattern, and could no more have left out the Agôn
or the Parabasis than he could leave out the phallic
dress. 'Could not' is perhaps a misleading expression: the truth probably is that the idea of
doing so would not occur to him any more than
a modern illustrator would think of drawing Punch
without a hump. We are usually unconscious of
those things which we do merely because they are
traditional, though, as taste changes, the tradition
changes too. The Agôn and Parabasis gradually
disappeared, as the phalli did. Punch's hump has
become so conventionalized that it hardly makes
the impression of a deformity.

Aristophanes' family belonged to the deme Kudathênaion in the heart of the city, though evidently he was accustomed to country life. The date of his birth is as uncertain as that of all his contemporaries. Babies are seldom famous. The ancient Life puts his *floruit* in the year 404, at the end of the Peloponnesian War, and, making the conventional assumption that he 'flourished' at the age of 40, concluded that he was born in 444. A rather earlier time would seem more probable, since his first play, the *Daitalês*, obtained a second prize in 427, and, though we know that he was young at the time, it is difficult to suppose that he was only 17. His own phrase is: 'I was still unmarried and could not lawfully bear a child; so I exposed my baby and another girl adopted it' (*Clouds*, 530). We know that he did not produce the play in his own name, but had it produced by a certain Callistratus, a practice which he often followed afterwards. His motives, however, are not quite clear. It looks as if there was either some legal limit of age which Aristophanes had not reached in 427, or else that he simply felt himself too young and inexperienced for producing a play and 'teaching a Chorus'. In any case, his action in 427 seems to have set up a habit, and frequently afterwards he employed either Callistratus or Philonides, of whom we know nothing but may guess that they were 'old hands', to do his productions for him. He apologizes for the practice in a passage of the *Knights*, quoted on the next page. It is partly that he feared the fickle public; partly that he believed in long apprenticeships.

Let us consider the personal situation in which the young man found himself. He remembered no Government before that of Pericles. As a child he had grown accustomed to the continued advances of the power of Athens; the founding of the great colonies at Thurii and Amphipolis, the conquest of Samos and Byzantium, the alliance with Corcyra in the Ionian Gulf, and with Rhêgion and Leontîni in Sicily. He had seen the outbreak of the Peloponnesian War: had suffered from the repeated invasions of Attica, and doubtless been driven, like the rest of the country population, to take refuge in the desperately over-crowded and under-housed city. When the Aeginetans were expropriated in 431 his family were given an estate in that island, but it can have afforded only a precarious refuge during the war.[1] He had lived through the plague of 430, which raged among the country refugees; through the death of Pericles and the succession of more violent and less educated men to the leadership of the people.

What were the first impressions made by the experiences of his adolescent years on this brilliant and sensitive boy, coming fresh from the peace and comfort and kindliness of country life into

[1] *Ach.* 653, with schol.; Theagenes περὶ Αἰγίνης.

the City with its splendour and its lack of food, its
bitterness and intrigue and all the atmosphere of
war? We can attempt an answer to this question
by a study of his first two plays. He was fascinated
by the comedies of his older contemporaries, of
whom he gives a brilliant and sympathetic account
in the parabasis of the *Knights* (507–44).

If one of the comedy-makers of old had attempted to
    order the Knights
To come forward and speak to the House in his name,
    we'd have said he exceeded his rights,
But this man really merits our help. He has hated the
    things we hate,
Defended the Right, and fronted the Storm, stood fast
    in the roaring Spate.
Now he tells us that dozens of people have come, and
    asked him, in some surprise,
Why he hasn't produced his plays himself, long ago,
    without any disguise.
Well, he wants us to say he has waited so long not for
    nothing, but—so he insists—
Because the production of Comedy is the most ticklish
    thing that exists.
Our fair Comic Muse is courted, he says, by hundreds,
    but smiles upon few.
Besides he had read your natures of old; you were
    annual plants, he knew,
You had never kept faith with the poets you loved; just
    used them and thrown them away.
He thought of what Magnês suffered, as soon as his
    temples began to be grey,
Though there never had been such a chorus as his, such
    a winner of prize upon prize,

Though he uttered all manner of varying sounds with
  his *Lutes* and his *Wings* and his *Flies*,
Though he talked like a *Lydian*, turned green like a
  Frog. Not enough! In the valley of years,
Though never in youth, he was hissed off the stage.
  'There was not enough life in his jeers!'
Of Cratînus he thought, at the height of his power, like
  a flood that burst through the level,
Till oaks, planes, enemies, up by the roots went
  flying, and off to the Devil;
When never a song at a banquet was heard but *Slipper
  of Silvery Tips*,
Or *Songful Grafters of Glutinous Palms*; 'twas a glory
  that none could eclipse.
And now, when you see him doddering past, for shame!
  have you nothing to say,
When he walks in a maze, like Connas of old, his lyre
  far gone in decay,
With the pegs dropping out, and the strings out of
  tune, and the joints of the framework burst,
The flowers of his garland of victory dead, and the old
  boy dying of thirst?
Why, if men had their rights, he should drink at his ease
  at the Hearth of Athena, and sit
Beside Dionysus here, clad in his best, in return for
  those glories of wit.
Then Cratês, too, what tempers of yours and buffetings
  he underwent!
Light lunches he gave you, at little expense, and dismissed you amused and content;
He made you the neatest confections of wit, well-
  phrased by the driest of lips;
He did—he only—hold out to the end, and stood—
  with occasional slips . . .

Their fate made him nervous, and willing to wait. And
    besides he was perfectly clear
That a sailor should first learn to pull at the oar, before
    he attempted to steer;
Then watch at the prow and examine the winds, and
    then, only then, take command!

There is real admiration in these lines, and it is
sad to think that we have almost no remains of the
poets criticized. We know that Magnês wrote
plays called the *Lydians*, the *Flies* (Ψῆνες), the
Harpers, the *Birds*, the *Frogs*. We have about
twenty-four whole lines of Cratês, and perhaps two
hundred of Cratînus, with more ingenious puns
about 'graft' and the 'slipping' of 'tips'. And we happen to know that these challenging lines had a decisive effect both on the public and on the drunken
old genius himself. He pulled himself together;
wrote a play about himself called the *Bottle* (Πυτίνη),
in which he at last extricated himself from the
wiles of the vamp, Methê, or Drink, and returned
to his true love, Comedy. And the public, repentant and hailing their old favourite's repentance,
gave him the first prize—above the *Clouds*!

Thus Comedy was a well-established traditional
form. It had existed from a time beyond the reach
of any living man's memory. It had received
public recognition and a place in the Great
Dionysia since Chionides won his first victory in
486. If Aristophanes was to attempt comedy at

all—and he found it as fascinating as it was difficult
—he must take it as it stood, with all its conventions; its double Chorus, its Agôn and Parabasis,
its phallic dress and saturnalian language, its final
Revel and Wedding. We can perhaps see from the
above verses what elements in it he was specially
likely to enjoy and develop; its poetry, its com-
bination of boisterous fun and refined wit, and its
outspoken comments on politics and manners.

He found he had something to say about these
last. He came, it would seem, from a highly cultivated home with a great knowledge of literature,
which meant at that time Homer, Hesiod, Pindar,
and the lyric poets, in general the great Ionian
tradition, together with the first fifty years or so
of Attic tragedy. His extant plays show that,
while Attic tragedy was his favourite subject, he
had all the higher literature at his fingers' ends.
He had further, it would seem, been brought up
in a somewhat old-fashioned gentlemanly style,
which laid stress on good manners, respect for the
aged, and conventional piety. He found in
Athens, the fevered and ambitious Athens of the
time, young men of his own age who were very
different in their outlook. Their morals were
much less strait-laced. Their general lack of rever-
ence disgusted him. They struck him as dread-
fully ignorant of Homer and good literature,
while they were very knowing about all sorts of
odd things that were strange to him. They knew

about police courts and laws and summonses, and political intrigues, and—apparently—problems of currency. Also they were full of strange information, and sometimes of shocking beliefs and disbeliefs, which they had learnt from the professional 'sophists' or men of learning.

Their language, in the first place, struck him as odd and affected. His earliest play, the *Daitalês*,[1] represents a father with two sons whom he has sent to be educated, one in the country and one in Athens. One fragment (198) gives a dialogue between the father and the city-bred youth. The offensive young man insults his father, and his father retorts by paying no attention to the substance of his remarks, but merely criticizing his vocabulary. 'You are half-dead', says the son; 'what are you but a coffin-song and perfume and funeral bands?', using the word σορέλλη for 'coffin-song'. 'Σορέλλη', says the father, 'that comes from Lysistratus.'[2] 'The years will soon floor you (καταπλιγήσει τῶι χρόνωι).' 'Καταπλιγήσει', says his father, 'you learnt that from the rhetoricians.' 'You will find these words come off (ἀποβήσεται).' Ἀποβήσεται comes from Alcibiades.' 'Why do

---

[1] The word Δαιταλεύς means 'banqueter' (A. *Prom.* 1024), but Galen (xix, p. 66) in quoting this play speaks of ὁ ἐκ τοῦ δήμου τῶν Δαιταλέων πρεσβύτης, so Aristophanes' Δαιταλῆς are evidently the people of the imaginary deme of that name; cf. Παλληνῆς, Μελιτῆς, &c. The suggestion is 'Plentyville' rather than 'Eatanswill'.

[2] Lysistratus, Χολαργεύς; *Ach.* 855; *Kn.* 1266; *Wasps*, 787, 1302; *Lys.* 1105.

you analyse my words (ὑποτεκμαίρῃ) and speak ill of
men who pursue the High-beautiful (καλοκἀγαθεῖν
ἀσκοῦντας)?' 'God help us, Thrasymachus!' (As one
might say, 'O shades of Lindley Murray!') 'What
orator deals in that monstrosity?' Every one of
the young man's affected words is imitated from
some one.

But for all his strange words, he does not know
the ordinary rudiments of poetry. 'What is the
meaning of κόρυμβα?' says another fragment.
'What are ἀμενηνὰ κάρηνα?' The youth does not
know these simple Homeric words, but he retorts
by asking if his virtuous brother knows the meaning of ἰΔυῖοι and ἀποινᾶν—legal terms used in
Solon's tables for 'witnesses' and 'ransom'.[1] He
and his friends, it would seem, can quote 'moun-
tains of law-suits and heaps of decrees' if they are
wanted (217). The father is determined to argue
the matter out; 'No pity shall deter me from washing this salt fish with all the dirt I know is in it'
(ὅσα συνοῖδ᾽ αὐτῷ κακά) (200, 201). The young
man defends himself cynically. 'Are you going to
sacrifice a puppy-dog to Hecate? Are you going
to invoke old Erechtheus and Aigeus against
me?' He knows how to change money (208), he
knows all about scents (205, 206). As for music,
he is helpless when asked to sing an ordinary

---

[1] Si lectio certa: ἰΔοῦσ᾽ and τὸ εὖ ποιεῖν MSS. There is a similar
scene in Antiphanes, *Aphrodisius*, fr. 52, where one of the speakers
talks in ultra-tragic phrases.

song of Alcaeus or Anacreon (223). He was sent
to the city, it would seem, to learn; but he has
learnt only to drink, to sing badly, to dine and
feast in the style of Syracuse and Sybaris, and to
ask for 'Chian wine in a Laconian jar' (216). His
father, and apparently the virtuous brother also,
took cold baths in the morning (ἐψυχρολουτήσαμεν,
237), and hard exercise afterwards. Not so he.
'I am utterly worn out with practising on your
flutes and lyres', he says, 'and now you want me
to dig' (221). What then has he done with himself
all this time? 'I shook the trees, I begged money,
I used threats, I made the figs drop' (ἔσειον,
ᾔτουν χρήματ', ἠπείλουν, ἐσυκοφάντουν, 219). By
these practical blackmailing arts he flourished, as
he could never have flourished by Homer and
Mousikê. He did no athletics, and had not even
a strigil or an oil-pot in his possession (207). He
was smooth like an eel, and—rather to our surprise—had golden ringlets!

These fragments come to us, of course, without
their context, and one can never be sure of inter-
preting them correctly. Some of the above suggestions may be quite wrong. But in general we
can get from these passages some picture of the
contrast which young Aristophanes felt between
his own country training and that which was
becoming fashionable in Athens under the influence of the war. War makes people bitterly and
brutally practical. What is the good of poetry or

music or culture of any sort, when the thing that
matters is, if possible, to win the war, but anyhow
to avoid starving or being killed, and meanwhile
to have as good a time as possible?

It seems probable, though evidence of course
fails us, that, with due allowance for exaggera-
tions, Aristophanes' account is true: war was already having its normal effect on character and
conduct, an effect perhaps helped onward by the
presence of the sophists and the general tendency
of the enlightened to despise the superstitions
of the ignorant. At any rate, the satire struck
the imagination of his contemporaries. 'My good
young man and dissolute young man were praised
very highly' (ἄριστ' ἠκουσάτην), he says in the
Clouds (529). The *Daitalês* was a success and the
first effort of the unknown youth was awarded a
second prize. He was encouraged, and ready for
a still bolder venture.

The year 427 saw the fourth invasion and
ravaging of Attica by the Peloponnesians. It saw
the outbreak of the savage civil war in Corcŷra,
which gives rise to some of the most terrible
chapters of Thucydides (iii. 70–85). It saw also
the final capture by the Athenians of the rebel city
of Mytilene, which surrendered without conditions. Cleon, 'the most violent of the citizens
and at that time the most influential with the
people', came forward at this crisis to preach his
doctrine of 'mass terror'. The Athenian allies were

subjects, not friends, much less fellow-citizens. If they were faithful they were faithful through fear; if they turned false, they must be made an example to strike terror into all the rest. He proposed that the whole adult male population of Mytilene without exception should be put to death. Then Athens could breathe freely, since in the other cities which might be disaffected every single man would know that any rebellion, even if he abstained from joining it, would mean his own execution. Cleon carried the day. A ship was sent off to Mytilene bearing to the general there these ghastly orders.

Then, we are told, the Assembly changed its mind, and we hear much about the fickleness of the Attic democracy. When we reflect that the citizens of Athens numbered at this time quite 35,000, and that an attendance of 5,000 at the Assembly was considered a record (Thuc. viii. 72), a better explanation suggests itself. Only a fragment of the population attended the Assembly. Probably on the whole those who liked hearing Cleon attended, those who disliked it stayed away. The first Assembly passed Cleon's motion, but when the news of it got out among the mass of average decent citizens there was a general feeling of horror. It was difficult but not absolutely impossible to hold another Assembly forthwith and to try to get the decree rescinded. Thucydides tells us how this was done, how Diodotus defeated

Cleon, and how a second ship bearing the reprieve
set off on the heels of the first; how the men rowed
at high speed in relays without resting and, since
the first ship had travelled slowly and with a heavy
heart, just arrived in time to stop the massacre.
Only the 'most guilty' (οἱ αἰτιώτατοι) were
actually put to death. The number is uncertain.
If we think over this story we can see what a
tempest of emotion must have raged at Athens.

One Athenian, at any rate, flinched from no
danger and counted no cost. In the spring of the
following year, at the Great Dionysia, late in April
when the seas were navigable and the concourse of
visitors to Athens from all the allied communities
was at its height, the young Aristophanes produced the *Babylonians*. It seems to have been a
thoroughgoing attack on the whole policy of the
'tyrant City' towards its allies and dependants.
He attacked, says the Scholiast (*Ach.* 378), 'all the
Athenian officials, whether elected or chosen by
lot, and above all, Cleon'. The real Babylonians
had rebelled against Darius and been reduced with
exceptional and famous cruelty (Hdt. iii. 150 ff.).
In this play the Allied Cities formed a Chorus of
Babylonian slaves working at the mill: worse, they
were branded slaves; 'That is the people of Samos,
covered with letters', observes some one, as he sees
the slaves trooping out from the mill, and ancient
authorities tell us that the poet was referring to an
actual outrage committed by the Athenians many

years before, when they branded their Samian prisoners in the war of 440 (fr. 64).[1]

The interpretation of the fragments is difficult. One line describes 'a man in fetters carrying a shield'—How could the Allies fight effectively for Athens when they were in fetters? (65). Another fragment shows a soldier demanding billets and commenting on the good furniture of a house (72, 73). Perhaps such furniture was considered too good for mere islanders, and was forthwith looted? Another shows the extortioner saying 'I need 200 drachmae'. 'But how am I to get them?' asks his victim. 'In this pint pot', is the reply. There is mention of corruption and bribery at Athens (81), and of some one—was it an Athenian soldier?—killing some islander's yoke of plough oxen because he wanted beef (82). We can to a great extent fill in the details of the attack made in this lost play from the more discreet repetition of it in the *Knights*.

Considering what war-neuroses are, even in a modern society; considering the power of Cleon, the scarcely avoided massacre of Mytilene, and the actual sufferings of Athens at the time, one can only marvel at the courage of the Archon Basileus who gave a Chorus to this production, of Callistratus the producer, and of the young poet

---

[1] It is possible that the decree περὶ τοῦ μὴ κωμῳδεῖν (τὴν πόλιν καὶ τὸν δῆμον), which was passed in 440, was due to the outburst of public indignation against the treatment of the Samians. Schol, *Ach.* 67, and Starkie, Excursus II. The decree was repealed two years later.

himself. It was an act of the same generous idealism which afterwards drove Euripides into exile
after the *Troades*, and inspired Thucydides to
write the Melian Dialogue. One wonders a little
that Aristophanes escaped with his life. He did
not get off scot-free. He was prosecuted,[1] apparently on a charge of alien birth, which broke
down, as well as on other grounds which we cannot
exactly define, but which seem to have included
the capital crime of ἀδικία εἰς τὸν δῆμον, or high
treason.

We have his own brief reference to it in the
Acharnians (377 ff.):

> And how Cleon made me pay,
> I've not forgotten, for my last year's play:
> Dragged me before the Council, brought his spies
> To slander me, gargled his throat with lies,
> Niagara'd me and slooshed me, till—almost—
> In so much sewage I gave up the ghost.

He certainly did not give it up altogether. Next
year at the winter festival he produced the *Acharnians*, which is on the one hand a definite plea for
peace, and on the other a defence of the author
against certain accusations. One may suppose that
a spectator of the *Babylonians* would say: 'This
man is slandering his country, choosing a time
when the Allies are present for the season to take

---

[1] The Ravenna Scholia say: Κλέων ἐγράψατο αὐτὸν ἀδικίας εἰς τοὺς
πολίτας, ὡς εἰς ὕβριν τοῦ δήμου καὶ τῆς βουλῆς ταῦτα πεποιηκότα. They add
καὶ ξενίας δὲ αὐτὸν ἐγράψατο καὶ εἰς ἀγῶνα κατέστησεν. The first charge seems
to have been ἀδικία εἰς τὸν δῆμον.

their side against Athens, and make them think that Athenian opinion is divided, thus showing himself a traitor and a pro-Spartan.' He answers in the *Acharnians*: 'This is the Lenaea, the winter feast, when there are no strangers present, so I am free to say what I like. I am not attacking the City (οὐχὶ τὴν πόλιν λέγω), I am attacking certain scoundrelly individuals. I hate the Spartans and wish them all misfortune, but I do say that on certain points we do them wrong and accuse them falsely. But above all, the way to get rid of all our troubles is not to argue about rights and wrongs but to make peace!'

The *Acharnians* is comparatively reticent about Cleon. Presumably Aristophanes wanted a breathing space, but naturally enough people were found who accused him of having been bullied into subservience. (*Wasps*, 1284: 'there are people who said I had made terms when Cleon fell upon me and shook me; little I care'.) There are some five passing references.[1] For example, the hero mentions that one of the pleasures of the year has been the sight of Cleon—apparently in some play or other—being made to 'disgorge the five talents'; and the Chorus speak of hating some one 'worse than Cleon, whom I mean to cut up into leather strips for the Knights', or, by a secondary meaning, 'in the *Knights*', i.e. in the play of that name. These are just enough to show that Aristo-

[1] *Ach.* 6; see Starkie's Excursus I: ib. 300 ff.

phanes is not reconciled. He has not been bought
off. But for the rest there is little attack on Cleon,
and the leader of the war party is the decent
soldier, Lamachus.

Yet the *Acharnians* is an extremely daring play.
The hero is a typical Aristophanic figure, an Old
Farmer, with a name—Dicaiopolis—that means
'Honest Citizen', and with an amount of wit
and of literary culture that can hardly have been
usual among farmers even in Attica. At the opening of the play Dicaiopolis is waiting in the Agora
in a highly uncivic state of mind, prepared to
insist on a discussion of Peace, and to interrupt all
orators who talk about any other subject. The
Assembly fills up, late as usual, and everybody
jostling for a place, when there enters among the
crowd a Demigod—or, as we might say, an Arch-
angel—Amphitheos, descended from Dêmêtêr and
Triptolemus, who explains that the gods have
entrusted him alone with the duty of making peace
with the Lacedaemonians. Unfortunately, however, he has not enough money to pay his fare and
the authorities will not. . . . 'Police!' calls the
Herald, and the unfortunate Demigod who dared
to mention Peace is bundled off, while the
Assembly proceeds to interview the Ambassadors
who have returned from Persia bringing with
them a high Persian officer, called the King's Eye,
who is expected to finance the next campaign.
(Incidentally they have had two years away from

the war, with pay at the rate of two drachmas a
day all the time.) Meanwhile Dicaiopolis has met
the Demigod, given him his fare to Sparta, and
instructed him to bring back Peace for Dicaiopolis and his family—alone. There is a play on
words here, or rather a pretended misunderstanding. The gods, says Amphitheos (51, 52), 'have
entrusted the task of bringing back Peace from
Sparta *to me alone*'. 'Then bring it', says Dicaiopolis, '*to me alone*' (131). The Assembly continues, interviews some preposterous mercenaries
from the King of Thrace, and is dismissed, when
the Demigod returns running for his life. He has
been seen by some charcoal-burners and farmers
of the deme Acharnae, who want the blood of the
wicked pacifist. For the moment, however, he
seems to have escaped from them. Dicaiopolis
chooses among the peace-libations that the Demigod has brought those that are good for Thirty
Years, and proceeds to gather his wife, daughter,
and two slaves to celebrate the Feast of Dionysus
in the Fields—the feast that could never be held
till Peace came. It is a phallic feast, the slave carrying the symbol on a pole, and the daughter—we
are specially told—looking demure and seemly.
In the midst of it in rush the Acharnian charcoal-
burners, put an end to the festival and threaten to
kill the traitor who has made peace with those to
whom 'no faith, no oath, no altar' is sacred.
Dicaiopolis begs them to listen while he shows that

the Lacedaemonians are not the cause of all their troubles. 'Not all? Not all?' they cry in rage; and he perseveres. 'No, not all; and in certain points they have been unfairly treated!' With difficulty he gets permission to speak, but only to speak with his head over a block, so that he may be instantly put to death if he does not convince his audience.

This is an astonishing scene. It would have been quite impossible in any country of Europe during the late war, for a writer, however brilliant, to make a speech on behalf of the enemy in a theatre before an average popular audience. He could write a pamphlet. He could address a small meeting of those who agreed with him; but he could never make a defence of the enemy and an attack on the national policy in the midst of a performance in a national theatre. And if impossible in our time, it would scarcely have been possible in any other period of history. This is one of the points in which Athens definitely reached a higher level of toleration than any other society known to us. Dicaiopolis is naturally anxious—and Aristophanes, one would image, no less so. In an extremely funny scene he determines, in order to work upon the Acharnians' feelings, to call upon Euripides and borrow the dress and make-up of one of his most pathetic heroes. Then, dressed like the wounded and outcast prince, Têlephus, he comes up to the block and speaks. His speech is

worth studying. It is not of course a careful
historical statement: that would be out of place.
It is not pro-Spartan; it begins by an utter re-
pudiation of any such feeling. It is a fair and
persuasive argument that the war has arisen out
of a muddle and is a very bad way of correcting
the muddle.

'We are alone here, all pure-blooded Athenians,
so I can say what I like.—I hate the Spartans all
right. My vines have been cut down as much as
yours. But why blame the Spartans for everything?
You know there is a tariff against Megarian goods.'
(It was a cruel tariff, but he does not dwell on that.
He blames an unpopular class, the informers.)
'There is a tariff, and a pack of scoundrelly informers were always worrying the Megarians.
Every article they could find was Megarian, and
was confiscated on the spot. Then outrages began
across the frontier. Some drunken young Athenians carried off a Megarian girl. The Megarians
carried off two girls'—he says, 'two whores', but
that is only his way of being agreeable—'belonging
to Aspasia. Then Pericles the Olympian

Roared, thundered, lightened, and confounded Greece;
Composed a law, more like a drinking piece,
That "never more by sea or shore", or sky,
Or market, should Megarians sell or buy.

The Megarians were reduced to starvation and
appealed to Sparta. What else could they do?
The Spartans made an application to Athens to

have the decree rescinded. What else could they do? We refused. They applied again and again, and we still refused. And then came the rattling of shields! "That was wrong of them", you say? Well, say what would have been right? Suppose some Lacedaemonian informer had gone out in a boat and confiscated a puppy dog belonging to your smallest island, would you have stood it? You know you would not. You would have launched three hundred ships on the spot.—And we do not expect the Lacedaemonians to do the same? Then there is no sense in us!'

I think the answer of the Periclean party to this speech would have been: 'Thus put, the policy of Athens sounds absurd. But these trifles were only the occasion of the war. The causes were the deep and growing rivalry between Athens and Sparta. The war was inevitable, it was only a question of choosing the time.' To which Aristophanes might have replied: 'It is no defence of a silly action to prove that it comes from a profound and inveterate lunacy. If you and the Lacedaemonians really went to war because you always wanted to, and just chose the first suitable pretext, you are even worse than I thought. War advantages nobody, and the only sensible thing is to make peace.'

However, to return to the play: the Chorus after this speech splits into two parties, for and against Dicaiopolis. His opponents, needing a champion, shout for Lamachus, who comes on in full armour with shield and flaming plumes. The argument between him and Dicaiopolis takes a new shape, though one that is generally familiar enough in war time.

'Who are you?' asks the bedizened officer.

'I? An honest citizen, not a place-hunter; one who has done his service ever since the war began, while you have had a place and a salary.'

'I was duly elected. . . .'

'By three cuckoos! It makes me sick to see grey-haired men in the ranks and young men, like you, escaping service by getting special missions and jobs.'

It is not clear what office Lamachus held. He was not a general at this time. But, like other holders of salaries and titles which depend on the war, he is determined to fight the Lacedaemonians to the bitter end. Dicaiopolis retorts by asserting that he personally is now at peace and by proclaiming a free market for the Peloponnesians, Megarians, and Boeotians—but not for Lamachus, since he prefers to be at war.

Here follows the parabasis. It is interesting to study exactly what services the poet considers he has done. He comes forward only to defend himself. 'It is not true that he mocks at Athens and insults the people (629 ff.). On the contrary, he has saved you from being bamboozled by foreign speeches . . . like those of the King's Eye and

Sitalces. . . . Before he came, if ambassadors from the cities spoke of "Athens the violet-crowned", you sat up smiling with pleasure; they spoke of "Athens the Shining", and you gave them whatever they asked . . . "for a compliment that applies equally to sardines!" In this way he has served you well, and also by showing the Allied Cities how your demos governs them! So now they come flocking with their tribute, eager to see the best of poets, who has dared to tell the Athenians the truth. . . . So let Cleon say what he likes, and plot as he likes, against me, for the right is on my side.' This claim is easy to understand, and is boldly made. The only other point raised in the parabasis is a curious one: a complaint that old men are badly treated. Smart young orators bring charges against them in the courts and browbeat them and bewilder them, as was done in particular to the old aristocratic leader Thucydides, son of Melêsias. This agrees with the picture drawn in the *Daitalês*, where the corrupt young man knows all the tricks of the law and practises blackmail, but curiously enough it seems contrary to the *Wasps*, where the old men are devoted to Cleon and the law-courts while the other side is represented by young Bdelycleon. In this play too the fierce Acharnians are old men, 'veterans of Marathon, hard as oak'. Perhaps the solution is that while the old men are full of warlike spirit and form severe juries, the dissolute younger generation provide the smooth and tricky orators who badger and entrap the prisoners, especially if they are old and unready, or, of course, if they come from the islands.

After the parabasis Dicaiopolis sets up his market. The first arrival is a Megarian. He and his are starving, and he has nothing to sell except his two daughters, whom he puts in a bag and tries to pass off as pigs. It is a farcical scene, with an appeal to pity behind the farce. 'What do you do in Megara?' 'We play starving matches round the fire.' 'How are politics?' 'We have appointed a special commission to find the quickest and worst road to ruin.' 'How is corn?' 'Prized like the blessed Gods.' 'Do you bring salt, then?' 'You have all the salt.' 'Garlic, then?' 'Garlic? Why, when you invade, you root up every plant of garlic with a peg.' Dicaiopolis buys the pigs, and runs at once to get them peas and figs to eat, and sees that the father also picks up a few. The Megarian is departing comforted, when in comes an informer, who is proceeding to confiscate both the pigs and the sack, when Dicaiopolis, as Overseer of the Market, thrashes him out of the place.

The next visitor is a great contrast, a Boeotian farmer, laden with all manner of good things, and preceded by some excruciating pipers. He brings a large and extremely mixed bag: ducks, choughs, francolins, coots, wrens, divers, geese, hares, moles, hedgehogs, weasels, brocks, martens, otters, and

Copaic eels. Dicaiopolis' enthusiasm knows no
bounds; his beloved eel, whom he has not seen for
years, and with whom he would live and die, as
Admetus with Alcestis in Euripides play:

> Oh, not in death from thee
> Divided, in a beet-root fricassee!

(Admetus had said: 'who alone art true to me'.)
But how is he to pay for it? Everything he can
suggest is plentiful in Boeotia already, and the
Boeotian wants something purely Attic. At this
moment there arrives again the Informer, a real
inimitable Attic product! 'It is rather small', complains the Boeotian; 'But all of it bad', says Dicaiopolis comfortingly. The Informer is seized, tied
up in a matting like a pot, to prevent his breaking,
and carried off carefully upside down—quite safe
though a little noisy.

Other applicants arrive. A servant of Lamachus,
who wishes to buy some game and an eel; a weeping farmer who has lost his yoke of oxen by a
Boeotian invasion, and wants a drop of peace
poured into his eyes; a bridegroom's best man;
all are refused till a bridesmaid comes to whisper
an extremely private request from the bride. She
is a woman and not responsible for the war (1062)
—it is interesting to find Aristophanes already
striking that note—so her prayer is granted.

Then come two messages; an invitation for
Dicaiopolis to dine with the Priest of Dionysus,
a summons from the Generals to Lamachus to

start at once for a campaign. Dicaiopolis prepares
for his feast and Lamachus for his march in the
snow, each making comments on the other meanwhile. After the next Choral Song, Lamachus is
borne back wounded amid lamentations, which
correspond metrically with the intoxicated rejoicings of Dicaiopolis, who comes back in the arms
of two young women, in a wild and unedifying
Kômos-Gamos. The ritual of the original Dionysiac feast reasserts itself, and—however startling to
modern taste—saves the comic poet from being
altogether too priggish and high-toned a preacher.
A public entertainer who preaches to his audience
must take care lest they think him a bore and a
scold. And Aristophanes has run some risks in this
play. They might well treat him as a traitor, if
they could not laugh him off as a mere buffoon.

CHAPTER II

CLEON
(*Knights*, *Peace*)

IN the *Acharnians* we have seen the first bold statement of Aristophanes' case for peace as against war. We have noticed that in that play the poet was almost silent about Cleon, but significantly promised that he was going to deal with him in a future play which he had already conceived and named the *Knights*. The *Acharnians* was produced in February 425, at the Lenaea. The *Knights* was to follow at the same time next year. But in the meantime Cleon, already 'the most violent of the citizens and most influential with the people' (Thuc: iii. 36), had acquired an immense addition to his power. A picked force of Spartans of the best families had been isolated on the island of Sphacteria, and the Athenians were besieging them there in the orthodox manner. Things moved slowly and Cleon in the Assembly kept denouncing the incompetence of the generals, Nicias and Demosthenes. 'If they were men', he said, 'they would have captured or killed the whole Spartan force before this. That is what he would do if he were general.' Goaded beyond the limits of his patience, Nicias suddenly resigned his command and proposed that Cleon should take it. The proposal was approved by the Assembly. Cleon had to accept, and braving the matter out, swore to bring the Spartans in, dead or alive, in twenty days. The boast seemed mad, says Thucydides, but by a freak of fortune was actually fulfilled. A forest fire left the island denuded of cover; the Spartans were found to be much weaker than had been supposed, and Demosthenes was a daring and able commander. Within twenty days the Spartans were captured and Cleon came home in triumph, having shown that 'the most violent of the citizens' was also the most successful of the generals. Would Aristophanes dare to persist in his attack?

He did. He attacked with a whirlwind of invective and an utter contempt for personal consequences. He is said to have had some help from his colleague or rival, Eupolis; and he must have had support from the Archon Basileus or some of the authorities of the festival. But it was a bold thing for a young man with no official position to challenge the greatest man, and one of the most unscrupulous, in Athens to a battle of life and death. In reading the *Knights* we are subject to a common illusion. The daily perils of the time are dead and forgotten; political issues are dimly conjectured; while the gibes and jests are full of life and entirely occupy the mind of the reader. We laugh as we read the passage where Cleon thrusts himself overbearingly forward and the offal-monger gets in his way (338–41):

CLEON. Allow me!

OFFAL-MONGER.   No!

CLEON.   Allow me!

OFFAL-MONGER.   No! You shan't address them first.

CLEON. (Oh, I shall burst!) ALLOW ME!

OFFAL-MONGER.   NO!

CHORUS. Oh, please, Sir, let him burst!

The gallant laughter lives for us, but we forget the tragedy, or threat of tragedy, that lay beneath it. We think of Cleon as a violent, vulgar, raging upstart and see him suitably confounded by a rival as vulgar as himself and far more witty. We read jokes about food, about informers, about rich islanders to be squeezed, about people who vomit from fear if Cleon looks at them, and we hardly appreciate the facts because we are so beguiled by the words.

In the first place we should realize Cleon's actual power. He bestrides Greece like a colossus, one leg in Pylos and one in the Athenian Assembly (75). He is an eagle hovering in the air (197 ff.). The rich dread him, and the poor gibber at the sight of him (223 ff.). When Aristophanes wanted to represent him on the stage the mask-makers struck: they did not dare to do it[1] (230). He counts the people as his property (714). He fears nothing 'as long as the Council lives and the People sits spell-bound upon the Pnyx' (395). He has now every civic honour, the right to dine

----

[1] It is said (Schol. *Eq.* 230, and Second Argument, also the *Life*) that Aristophanes played the part himself.

in the Prytaneum, and other exceptional distinc-
tions which not even Pericles had enjoyed before
(283). He compares himself to Themistocles!
(812). And in answer to every criticism there
comes a reference to his great victory at Pylos—
almost enough in itself to win the war! (55, 702,
742, 1052, 1058, 1201).

A great part of Aristophanes' attack consists in
the commonplaces of ancient political invective.
In a society where advocates and political speakers
were not clearly separated, and fees not regulated
by an authorized tariff, every advocate who took
a fee was apt to be accused of 'graft'. There is
reason to think that Cleon, for all his political
power and success, was never a rich man, and we
need not pay too much attention to the constant
accusations of theft and corruption (296, 403,
444, 1219), nor to the supposed five talents that
he had to disgorge (*Ach.* 6). Indeed, Aristophanes
almost admits the truth of Cleon's own defence;
ἐγὼ 2' ἔκλεπτον ἐπ' ἀγαθῷ γε τῇ πόλει (1226), 'I
only stole in the interest of the City'. It is not
theft or personal corruption with which Cleon is
charged; it is extortion and political blackmail.
That is why the rich dread him; that explains
why he anticipates revenue by seizing taxes before they are due (258 ff.) and keeps an eye on
all officials to see if he can get damages out of
them. He stands on the rock, watching the seas
like a cormorant, or like a tunny-fisher, ready to

pounce upon the tribute from the Allied Cities
(313). He is a slaver, a kidnapper, who goes
round at night licking up whatever is left on the
islands (1030). This explains the celebrated meta-
phor of the eel-fisher, who catches most in troubled
waters: Cleon likes war and confusion because his
irregularities cannot be detected (864).

Cleon practically admits these charges. He is
not ashamed of them. His business was to win the
war, and during the war to keep the Demos of
Athens from starving, and he did it. 'When I was
counsellor I produced the largest store in the
treasury by torturing here, and squeezing there,
and begging somewhere else—caring nothing for
any man as long as I could make the Demos
happy!' (773). 'I may shout indifferently for
right or for wrong, but I keep you fed by it!'
(256). The incident in the Agora (642-82) illustrates this. The news that a shoal of anchovies had
come into the Piraeus, and that fish was to be had
cheap, sets up a scene of enthusiasm and empties
the market-place, a thing which could only have
occurred among a half-starved population. The
same fact makes us understand Cleon's attempt to
win back the Assembly's attention by a large
sacrifice and its consequent distribution of meat.
The Offal-monger, by announcing the shoal of
anchovies, has beaten Cleon at his own game. He
has provided food for the people.

This is Cleon's main defence. The Demos had

to be fed, and he could feed them . . . by whatever means. '*Que mon nom soit flétri*', he might have said with Danton, '*que la Cité soit sauvée.*' But he had some other pleas too. He will carry the Demos through all its trials, 'providing in some good blackguardly way (εὖ καὶ μιαρῶς) a constant supply of three-obol bits, till at the end it attains the empire of all Hellas'. That is why he rejects all overtures of peace. That is why he urges the people not to grumble at living in sentry-boxes and huts and tubs; that is why he establishes his reign of terror over all the rich, and especially the rich of the Allied Cities, who have not the full civic rights. As to his use of blackmailers and informers, he would say, how could he do without them? Such a government as his exasperated the rich and the Allies, and they were always conspiring against the Demos (862, 462, 435 ff., 278). The συκοφάνται were a necessity, and he protected them.

One plea, perhaps, Cleon can really make good, since it rests on Aristophanes' own evidence. And it is an important one. In the *Frogs* two poor women, an Innkeeper and her maid, have been robbed and believe that they see the man who robbed them. Their first thought is to appeal to Cleon. He will see them righted. In New York such a woman would appeal to Tammany. Friends of the injured poor are not always persons of high character, especially in times of war or revolution.

Yet to be a friend of the injured poor is a thing of
which Cleon might justly be proud, even if it does
not constitute a defence against other charges.

Another plea which Cleon puts forward is of
some historical interest. The homosexual attach-
ments of which we hear a good deal in Greek
literature were originally a regular military insti-
tution implying a high degree of duty and devotion; as such they lived on in Sparta and in Crete,
and, though looked askance upon by Athenian
law,[1] were to some extent admired and imitated
by the Laconizing Athenian aristocrats. It was in
such circles that Plato preached his celebrated
doctrine of an Erôs which should be passionate but
purely spiritual. Cleon, representing the ordinary
plebeian sentiment, was hostile to all such ideas, and
claims to have put a stop to such practices in
Athens by striking off the roll of citizens some
guilty person of whom we know no more. Aristophanes, in the heat of altercation, says this was only
his love of meddling with dirt (πρωκτοτηρεῖν, 878),
but in general feeling on this point he and Eupolis
were on the same side as Cleon. They were fierce
against the smooth young exquisites whom they
accused of these practices.[2]

We can get a little further by observing the
projects of reform proposed at the end of the play,

---

[1] Ἑταίρησις by a male involved the loss of all civic rights (ἀτιμία).

[2] ἔπαυσα τοὺς βινουμένους says Cleon, *Kn.* 877: cp. Eupolis, fr. 100;
Athen., p. 601 E.

when the Offal-monger, like another Medea, has
boiled Demos and made a new man of him. Demos
will no longer listen to mere flattery. He will no
longer spend on μισθός, or as we should say, on
'the dole', the money that ought to be spent on
the fleet (1350). [It is difficult to think that
Cleon, the war-monger, made this particular mistake.] He will no longer allow an advocate to say
to the jury: 'If you do not condemn this man
and confiscate his property there will not be bread
for you to eat!' If a man says such a thing, vows
the repentant Demos, I will lift him up and fling
him into the Pit,[1] with a Hyperbolus—the heaviest
of the informers—hung round his neck! Such
a plea was not uncommon in the French Revolution and probably occurs in all revolutions. We
hear it mentioned in Lysias, 27. 1 (cf. 30. 22);
while Aristotle (*Pol.* vii (vi) 5) counts such confiscations among the worst dangers of democracy.
Cleon, of course, was a great hand at confiscations.
He knows all the rich and harmless men who have
held any office and are therefore exposed to blackmail (260 ff.).

The regenerate Demos will see that the sailors
get their pay. Cleon, apparently, had left them to
live on the islanders (1066). When in difficulties
he would demand warships for collecting arrears
of tribute and send them out to collect—with no
questions asked.

[1] Penalty for ἀδικία εἰς τὸν δῆμον.

The last reform promised by Demos is fair play
in respect of military service. No names shall be
taken out of the muster-roll by private influence,
and the young newfangled loungers in the Agora
shall be suppressed and compelled to take hard
exercise. These μειράκια were no friends of Cleon,
nor, perhaps, of any one else; and the last reform
would be generally popular with the Attic multitude. The spending of revenue on the fleet instead
of the jury-fees was, if not exactly popular, at any
rate accepted as right. But most of the reforms
are in the interest of a great population which was
not present in Athens at the Lenaea and is not
mentioned until the very last word of the play. In
the *Babylonians* Aristophanes had pleaded openly
and passionately the cause of the Allies, always
absent, always voteless, and consequently easy to
oppress. He had got into trouble and danger. In
this attack on Cleon in the *Knights*, while he piles
up the list of Cleon's iniquities one feels that most
of the suffering they cause falls on the Allies,
especially the quiet and well-to-do families who
still represented the old Ionian literary culture.
But they are not openly championed. Only in the
last scene, when sentence is pronounced on Cleon
—not death, not banishment: only that he shall
go to the trade that he is fit for, sell sausages of
dog's flesh and asses' flesh at the Gates, drink and
curse and swear among the prostitutes that haunt
there, and drink the water out of the public baths

—only there, in the last word of the last line of the play, is their name mentioned: 'Up with him on your shoulders, to be a sight for those whom he wronged, the Allies.'

ἵν' ἴδωσιν αὐτὸν οἶς ἐλωβᾶθ', οἱ ξένοι.[1]

Thus the main position of Aristophanes in the *Knights* can be clearly understood. The issue between him and Cleon is the same as that which lay between Cleon and Diodotus in the great Mytilenean debate in Thucydides (iii. 37–48), though neither side there was able to state it clearly. Thucydides tells us straighforwardly that after the carrying of Cleon's proposal, 'Next day there came a change of feeling; people thought again and realized how cruel and momentous (ὠμὸν καὶ μέγα) the decision was: they demanded a new discussion of the subject, and the authorities, seeing clearly that a majority of the people wanted it, broke the law and called another assembly.' It was ὠμὸν καὶ μέγα: we know the connotation of μέγα in such a context. A μέγα ἔργον is a crime that stands out and cannot be forgotten. On that issue we have the two speeches, each typifying a different kind of patriotism.

Cleon's position is simple. He wants Athens to win the war, and he believes in nothing but force. 'Your allies do not follow you from love, but from fear. Therefore see that the fear is overwhelm-

[1] Cf. also 1319, ταῖς νήσοις ἐπίκουρε.

ingly strong.' It is so plain a case that the view
of his opponents puzzles him. Perhaps they are
bribed; that he could understand—just as the
popular press in England or France or Germany
during the War thought all moral scruples and all
criticisms of the war party were due to bribery.
But somehow they were not the kind of people
who were likely to be bribed. The truth was,
they were 'intellectuals'—and when people once
go in for intellect God knows what may happen
to them! They want to be τῶν νόμων σοφώτεροι,
'wiser than the laws'. That is why stupid people
manage public affairs much better than clever
ones.[1] The intellectuals make fine speeches, but
are not practical. They do not understand the real
world—which is ruled by force and fear—and are
always looking for ἄλλο τι ἢ ἐν οἷς ζῶμεν, 'something other than the life we live in'. They appeal
to 'pity, beauty of language and generosity . . . the
three most fatal enemies of Empire.[2] If they want
to practise virtue (ἀνΔραγαθίζεσθαι) for Heaven's sake
let them abandon politics and do it in a vacuum.'

How was Diodotus to answer these arguments?
By appeals to sentiment and denunciations of
cruelty? That would have been to play Cleon's
game, and to admit the truth of his argument.
Diodotus in Thucydides takes the obviously wise
course. The people who were moved by pity were

[1] οἱ φαυλότεροι τῶν ἀνθρώπων πρὸς τοὺς ξυνετωτέρους ὡς ἐπὶ τὸ πλέον ἄμεινον
οἰκοῦσι τὰς πόλεις, iii. 37.

[2] τρισὶ τοῖς ἀξυμφορωτάτοις τῇ ἀρχῇ, οἴκτῳ καὶ ἡδονῇ λόγων καὶ ἐπιεικείᾳ, iii. 40.

on his side already, what he had to do was to show
that the policy of mercy was also the policy of wise
self-interest for Athens, and it is on that that he con-
centrates. The debate none the less illustrates one
of the eternal issues which arise in great national
emergencies between two types of patriotism: the
simple brutal Cleonian type which just wishes its
own side to win and will do anything in the world
for the sake of any advantage; and the higher
type, which has a certain ideal for its city or
nation, and cares more for the maintenance of that
ideal than for this or that temporary gain. Cleon
was ready to terrorize the Allies, to pervert justice
in the courts, to extort money from innocent
people by false accusations or sheer robbery, in
order to make Athens the ruler of Hellas. Aristophanes loathed the whole spirit of such proceedings, he loathed the cruelty, the injustice, the
vulgarity and ignorance which he saw dominating
the public life of Athens. It was a different Athens
that he loved and served.

There is a startling inconsistency in the plot of
the *Knights*. It begins with a conspiracy of two
decent slaves—got up to resemble the generals
Nicias and Demosthenes—in the house of a crusty
old man called Demos; they can no longer stand
the intrigues and cruelty of his brutal Paphlagonian favourite—who represents Cleon. The
Paphlagon is a 'leather-monger'; as leader of the
people he has succeeded a rope-monger and a

mutton-monger; and an oracle is discovered announcing that his reign shall not pass away till
another 'monger' is found, to out-Cleon Cleon.
A 'black-pudding-man' or 'offal-monger' turns up
who satisfies these conditions. His name Ἀγοράκριτος,
though only used in the latter part of the play,
seems to mean 'Market-chosen', or 'the choice of
the vulgar'. He is more dishonest, more uneducated, more impudent, more foul-mouthed, more
universally a guttersnipe, and he plunges at once
into a long and eventually successful struggle for
power with Cleon (125 ff.).

Demosthenes, who, it should be mentioned, is a
little drunk, has discovered a book of oracles which
Cleon had kept under his pillow.

DEMOSTHENES. You gory Paphlagōnian, you did well
　To keep this close! You feared the oracle
　About yourself.
NICIAS.　　　　　　About himself? Eh, what?
DEM. It's written here, man, how he goes to pot.
NIC. How?
DEM.　　　　How? This book quite plainly prophesies
　How first a Rope-monger must needs arise
　The fortunes of all Athens to control. . . .
NIC. Monger the first! What follows in the roll?
DEM. A Mutton-monger next our lord shall be. . . .
NIC. Monger the second! What's his destiny?
DEM. To reign in pride until some dirtier soul
　Rise than himself. That hour his knell shall toll.
For close behind a Leather-monger steals,
—Our Paphlagonian—snarling at his heels,
Niagara in his lungs, a beast of prey.

NIC. The Mutton-monger runs, and fades away
  Before him?
DEM.   Yes.
NIC.   And that's the end? The store
  Is finished? . . . Oh, for just one monger more!
DEM. There is one more, and one you'd never guess.
NIC. There is? What is he?
DEM.   Shall I tell you?
NIC.   Yes?
DEM. His fall is by an Offal-monger made.
NIC. An Offal-monger? Glory, what a trade! . . .
  Up, and to work! That monger must be found!
DEM. We'll seek him out.

> (*They proceed to go seeking, when they see a man with
> a pieman's tray hanging round his neck, selling offal.*)

NIC.   See, on this very ground,
  By Providence!
DEM.   O blessing without end,
  O, Offal-monger, friend and more than friend!
  To us, to Athens, saviour evermore! . . .
  This way!
OFFAL-MONGER. What's up. What are you shouting
  for?
DEM. Come here: come forward, and be taught by me
  Your splendid fate, your rich felicity!
NIC. Here! Take his tray off! Pour into his head
  The blessed oracles and all they've said.
  I'll go and keep my eye on Paphlagon. - (*Exit* NICIAS)
DEM. Come, my good man, put all these gadgets down.
  Kiss Earth our Mother and the gods adore.
O.M. There. What's it all about?
DEM.   O blest and more!
  Now nothing, but to-morrow Lord of All!
  O Prince of Athens the majestical. . . .

o.m. Look here, gents, can't you let me wash my stuff
  And sell the puddings? I've had more'n enough.
dem. Puddings, deluded being? Just look up.
  You see these rows and rows of people?
o.m.   Yup.
dem. You are their Lord and Master! You heaven-sent
  To people, market, harbour, parliament,
  To kick the Council, break the High Command,
  Send men to gaol, get drunk in the Grand Stand. . . .
o.m. Not me?
dem.   Yes—and you don't yet see it—you!
  Get up on . . . here, your old tray will do.
  See all the islands dotted round the scene?
o.m. Yes.
dem.   The great ports, the mercantile marine?
o.m. Yes.
dem.   Yes! And then the man denies he's blest!
  Now cast one eye towards Carthage in the west,
  One round to Caria—take the whole imprint.
o.m. Shall I be really happier with a squint?
dem. Tut tut, man! All you see is yours to sell.
  You shall become, so all the stars foretell,
  A great, great man.
o.m.   But do explain: how can
  A poor little Offal-monger be a man?
dem. That's just the reason why you are bound to grow,
  Because you are street-bred, brazen-faced and low.
o.m. You know, I don't know quite as I deserve. . . .
dem. You don't know quite? What means this shaken
             nerve?
  Some secret virtue? No?—Don't say you came
  Of honest parents!
o.m.   Honest? Lord, not them!
  Both pretty queer!

DEM.   O happy man and wife!
   To start your son so well for public life.
O.M. Just think of the eddication I ain't had,
   Bar letters: and I mostly learnt 'em bad!
DEM. The pity is you learnt such things at all.
   'Tis not for learning now the people call,
   Nor thoughtfulness, nor men of generous make.
   'Tis brute beasts without conscience. Come and take
   The prize that gods and prophets offer you.

   .   .   .   .   .   .

O.M. Of course I like them. But I can't see yet
   How ever I shall learn to rule a state.
DEM. Easy as lying! Do as now you do,
   Turn every question to a public stew;
   Hash things, and cook things. Win the common herd
   By sweet strong sauces in your every word.
   For other gifts, you have half the catalogue
   Already, for the perfect demagogue;
   A blood-shot voice, low breeding, huckster's tricks—
   What more can man require for politics?
   The prophets and Apollo's word concur.
   Up! To all Sleeping Snakes libation pour,
   And crown your brow, and fight him!
O.M.   Who will fight
   Beside me? All the rich are in a fright
   Before him, and the poor folk of the town
   Turn green and vomit if they see him frown.[1]

But at the end of the play when the Offal-monger
gets Demos in his power, his character changes.
Apparently he has only practised Cleon's arts in
order to destroy Cleon: once free, he reveals himself as a reformer and saviour of the State.

   [1] *Knights*, 125–224, reprinted from *Aristophanes and the War Party*
(Allen & Unwin, 1918).

OFFAL-MONGER. Now peace, and be still! A seal on
　　your lips! Let the witness-box echo no voices!

Shut be the gates of the Jurors' Courts, wherein this
　　people rejoices!

Let the Theatre sing for the news I bring, and welcome
　　a wondrous tale!

CHORUS. O star in the night to Athens the Blest, O help
　　of the Islands, hail!

Say what glad thing is this that you bring, and our
　　altars shall smoke in the street.

O.M. I have boiled your Demos in magical herbs, and
　　turned him from rotten to sweet!

CHOR. O worker of wonders! Where standeth he now,
　　or where hath he laid him down?

O.M. He dwells in the Athens of ancient days, in Her
　　of the violet crown.

CHOR. How can we look on him? How is he changed?
　　What like in carriage and dress?

O.M. As he was when he sat at Miltiades' side and with
　　great Aristîdes at mess.

But soon ye shall see him. There, hearken, above us
　　the Gates of the Rock unfold.

Uplift your voices and open your eyes on Athens, the
　　Athens of old,

The wonderful City, the City of song, true home of
　　our Demos! Behold!

CHOR. O shining Athens, O violet-crowned, O blest
　　all cities above,

Unveil to our eyes the Lord of the Greeks, the Lord
　　of the Land we love!

O.M. It is he, in the clean grave raiment of old, the
　　grasshopper bright on his crown,[1]

---

[1] An older generation of Athenians used golden buckles in the shape
of a grasshopper to bind their hair.

No longer he smells of balloting shells, but of Peace
and myrrh running down.
CHOR. All hail, O King over Hellas the Great, we
rejoice in thy joy! For again
Thy life is worthy of Athens and true to the Trophy
on Marathon plain.

(1316–34)

Thus what Aristophanes is seeking in his opposition to Cleon is an Athens uncorrupted by war,
an Athens which lives nobly as in the days of
Aristîdes the Just. It is, with individual variations,
the ideal of Thucydides and Euripides; it is derived
from that of Aeschylus and Herodotus, and it leads
by an historical process to that of Plato.[1]

The *Acharnians* was a bold plea for peace in the

---

[1] It is possible that this latter part of the *Knights* is, in whole or part,
the work of Eupolis. The Scholiast on *Kn.* 1291 says somewhat con-
fusedly that from 1288 on 'the parabasis is said to be by Eupolis', and
the difference of authorship might account for the inconsistency. The
whole subject is obscure. Eupolis in his *Baptae* says: 'I wrote his
Knights with our bald friend and made him a present of it' (fr. 78).
Aristophanes, on the other hand, says (*Cl.* 554): 'Eupolis dragged his
Maricâs on to the stage by turning my *Knights* inside out, as badly as you
would expect of him (κακὸς κακῶς).' The *Maricâs* was an attack on
Hyperbolus, as the *Knights* was on Cleon. It would seem that the two
playwrights had first taken up together the cause of the Allies against
Cleon, Eupolis in his *Poleis*, Aristophanes in the plays we know; they
had attacked Cleon together in the *Knights*; then Eupolis turned aside,
left Cleon alone, and fell upon the less formidable Hyperbolus, using
some of the ideas they had struck out in common. The two quarrelled,
and Aristophanes, left alone, had to make some sort of concessions to
Cleon. What then is the meaning of *Wasps*, 1284 ff.? 'I saw that
people only laughed at me when I was flayed alive by Cleon, and
watched to see if I would say something funny. Consequently I did,
slightly, in a small thing play the monkey. It is a case of "The stake
betrayed the vine" '. Does this refer to Eupolis' defection?

height of the war-fever, the *Knights* an uncom-
promising attack on the spirit of a war policy
which was still triumphant; it is interesting to compare with these the tone of the *Peace*, produced
three years later, at the Great Dionysia of 423,
when Brasidas and Cleon were both dead, and all
was ready for the Peace of Nicias. Peace is in the
air; the sense of common danger and common
disaster is forming a bond of union between the
hostile cities, and Aristophanes' play is almost as
much an idyll as a satire.

The *Peace* is perhaps rather a tame drama, with
neither the wit nor the fire of the *Acharnians*, but
there is a wider humanity about it and more poetry.
The plot is simplicity itself. Trygaios ('Mr.
Grapier'), the honest Aristophanic vine-grower,
having heard from the messenger in Euripides'
tragedy how Bellerophon on his winged steed
Pegasus rode up to heaven to demand of Zeus some
explanation of the manifold injustices of the world,
determines to imitate him. He has no winged
horse, but tries instead one of those enormous
Sicilian beetles—in the *Feasts* of Plato Comicus we
hear of one 'as big as a man'. He successfully
reaches heaven, where he is met with indignation
and horror by the porter, Hermes. 'Accursed one,
why have you come?' 'To bring you these pieces
of meat', answers Trygaios, and the hungry janitor
softens. Evidently there is 'food shortage' in
heaven as well as on earth. It appears, however,

that Zeus and the gods, in sheer disgust at the Greeks, have left Olympus and handed things over to Polemos (War). Polemos has buried his enemy, the Maiden Peace, in a deep pit, and is about to pound the cities of Greece in a mortar. His pestle, however, is broken, Hermes explains, and he has gone out to get a new one. Taking advantage of his absence, Trygaios summons all the Greeks, particularly the farmers, to drag the figure of Peace, more than life-size—a device laughed at by Eupolis, fr. 54—up out of the pit; they do so, then follows a Kômos and a Gamos and general rejoicing.

Many of the notes struck are already familiar to us. There is the same shortage of food. One of Trygaios' objects is to get bread for his daughters (120). The feast at the end is to be given to 'a people starved before' (1312). Poverty has made men dishonest; they steal more than they ever did (402).[1] There is the same complaint about cheating in the muster-roll; people with a 'pull' are let off their military service and poor farmers imposed upon (1179–86). There is the same picture of the blackmailers and their extortions. It is tersely put in a speech of Hermes: 'The politicians saw that the poor were weak and lacked bread, so they squeezed the fat rich islanders. They dropped on some one with the accusation that he sympathized

---

1 (120) ἄχθομαι ὑμῖν | ἡνίκ' ἂν αἰτίζητ' ἄρτον, πάππαν με καλοῦσαι. (1312) ἀλλ' ὦ πρὸ τοῦ πεινῶντες, ἐμβάλλεσθε τῶν λαγῴων. (402) κλέπται γάρ εἰσι νῦν γε μᾶλλον ἢ πρὸ τοῦ.

with Brasidas, and then you all flew at him and tore him, like a lot of little dogs. For the City, sitting in terror with cheeks blanched, swallowed greedily every slander they threw to her. And many people, seeing how the allies were flogged, stuffed the mouths of the informers with gold. So they grew rich, while Hellas was being made a desert without your noticing! And the hand that worked it all was a tanner's. . . .' 'Oh, stop! stop!' cry the Chorus. 'No word more about him; he belongs to your world now, not ours.' The tanner, of course, was Cleon, who was now dead (635-48).

But for the most part it is not the peace party in Athens, it is not even Athens herself, on whose behalf the poet pleads. It is Hellas. 'O Zeus, what would you do to our people? Put down your broom; sweep not Hellas to destruction' (58-63). Trygaios makes his adventure ὑπὲρ Ἑλλήνων πάντων (93), 'on behalf of all Greeks'. Zeus has handed the Greeks over to Polemos to work his will upon because he is sick of their quarrelling and their factious prayers. If the Lacedaemonians had a small advantage, it was all 'Now, by God, the little Attic rogue shall skip!' If Athens won a victory, and the Spartans made offers of peace, the offer was a trap. 'They'll come again if we hold fast!' So Hermes puts it, and Trygaios nods: 'Yes, that is just our style!' (204-20).

In the grimly effective scene where Polemos is preparing his mortar, he mixes cities hostile and

friendly to Athens indifferently together (236–
88): 'O Prasiai, thrice miserable and five times . . .
how you shall suffer to-day!' (Prasiai was a city
in the Peloponnese.) 'O Megara, Megara, what
tribulation for you, once for all mashed into
a salmagundi! O Sicily. : . .' Then he looks for
some Attic honey and Trygaios nervously begs
him to use some other sort. The Attic is so ex-
pensive. As soon as Polemos is gone—he goes to
make himself a pestle, since both the Athenian
pestle and the Spartan have been lost, i.e. Cleon
and Brasidas are both dead—Trygaios appeals to
all honest tradesmen—'O farmers, merchants, car-
penters, public craftsmen, resident aliens, Allies
and Islanders, O all the People', and a little later
comes the rare phrase "ὦ Πανέλληνες" (296 ff.).

When he comes to the opponents of Peace he
says little of politicians, though there is some
danger that 'the infernal Cerberus'—Cleon, of
course—may rise from his grave; and at one moment, when all the Cities are trying to pull Peace
out of the pit, Lamachus is found sitting on the
rope. The opposition comes in part from a taxi-
arch (say, a colonel) or a general; from some spear-
maker or shield-seller who wants an increased
demand for his wares, or from a slave who has
made all the preparations for running away (444–
51; cf. 545 ff.). Apart from such individual cases,
it is the Argives who are not pulling. They were
neutrals and did good business by selling food to

both sides (475 ff.). The Spartans are pulling hard
. . . though those who are keenest for peace, the
poor prisoners from Pylos, cannot get at the rope!
The unfortunate Megarians are of little use; they
are doing their best, poor souls, and grinning like
dogs, but they are weak with famine. (Aristophanes seems to have been haunted, as well he
might be, by the deliberate starvation of the
Megarians.) They are told to leave off. And then,
to our surprise, the Athenians also are told to leave
off: they spend all their strength in litigation with
one another and do not really pull. At last it is
seen that the only people who are honestly pulling, with one mind and no thought of anything
else, are the husbandmen—farmers, vine-growers,
olive-growers, and the like—who in all nations
equally are the first sufferers from the war. These
γεωργοί—land-workers—are left to pull alone, and
soon are successful. Peace appears, and the various
Cities, just as they are, with their wounds and
bandages and black eyes, dance around her laughing for joy, their enmities forgotten (475–542).

Peace was signed, so Thucydides tells us, immediately after the Great Dionysia. The audience
coming out from seeing this comedy were expect-
ing the news. It came within a few days, and the
cause for which the poet pleaded was already won
when the play was produced. That fact accounts
for the difference of tone between it and the
Acharnians or *Knights*. The poet is no longer

fighting against odds, with his back against a wall, and hence comes a certain flatness and lack of fire. In return there is in the *Peace* something idyllic. Trygaios longs to talk again to his vines, whom he has not seen for so many years. He longs for the sledge-hammer cleaned again and shining bright, and the pitchforks gleaming in the sun. He remembers the old happy life that Peace gave them long ago, the fruit cakes and the figs and the myrtles, the sweet fresh wine, 'the bed of violets beside the well', and the olives, the beloved olives!

There is not enough material in the play, not enough plot or incident or invention, with the result that the phallic element, the Kômos and Gamos, is rather overdone. After all, Kômos was in the air: Peace was at hand, with its real and almost wilder rejoicings. One may remember the revels of London on Armistice Night in 1918.

One or two other points may be noticed in passing. There is the usual series of uninvited and unwelcome guests who make their appearance as Trygaios prepares his feast. First, indeed, comes a sickle-maker, full of joy. He can sell his sickles now, whereas for years they have not been wanted. The sickle-maker is invited in; but he is followed by representatives of all the armament firms, the makers of Crests, of Breastplates, of Trumpets, Helmets, and Spears, who all have poor receptions and are left mourning the loss of their market (1198–1267). But the longest scene and the

severest treatment are reserved for Hierocles the
Prophet, a figure whom we have not had in the
earlier plays, though a similar oracle-monger will
receive similar treatment in the *Birds* later on
(*Birds*, 959 ff.). He is like one of the war-monger-
ing priests, more ferocious than any layman, who
are satirized by Erasmus or Voltaire. 'O miserable
men and blind, knowing not the mind of the
Gods!' he begins: 'Behold, men have made cove-
nants with angry-eyed apes, trembling gulls have
put their trust in the children of foxes!... 'Tis the
will of the blessed gods that ye cease not from war
till the wolf weds the lamb. . . . Never shall ye
make the crab walk straight! Never shall ye make
the sea-urchin smooth. Bakis deceiveth not. . . .'
And so on, and so on. 'And are we never to stop
fighting?' asks Trygaios. 'Are we to draw lots for
who goes deepest to the Devil, when we might
simply make peace and rule Hellas together?' But
the inspired and holy man takes no heed of argument. He demands a place at the banquet, and,
not getting it, snatches at the food, and is whipped
away (1052–1120).

There are two stories or historical statements
repeated in this play from the *Acharnians* and the
Wasps respectively. Hermes gives an account of
the origin of the war (603 ff.), not verbally identical with that in the *Acharnians* but practically on
the same lines. It all comes from Pericles' inhuman
blockade of Megara. No country could stand such

treatment. No great nation like the Spartans could
stand seeing their allies so oppressed. The motives
attributed to Pericles are personal and trivial in
both cases: that is part of the comic convention.
In the *Acharnians* he wanted to avenge a wrong
done to Aspasia. In the *Peace* he was afraid of
being prosecuted like his friend Phidias, and so
sought to make trouble. Such explanations are
not, I think, meant to be taken seriously. Pericles'
real motive was probably a desire to get command
of the isthmus so as to make Attica invulnerable to
a Spartan invasion; this could have been done, had
he been able to induce Megara to come into the
Athenian alliance. He tried to do so by a famine-
blockade, and failed. It was too cruel a policy to
be wise, and its cruelty is evidently what struck
Aristophanes. The starvation of Megara is a thing
he cannot forget.

In the parabasis of the *Peace* there is a feature
which also occurs in the *Wasps* and the second
edition of the *Clouds* itself, a complaint about the
ill success of the *Clouds*, and a general justification
of the poet's dramatic work. He has elevated
comedy from a vulgar mass of horse-play and
farce to the level of a great art. But above all he
takes credit for his courage and public spirit.

At women and poor little private men he never mocked
  nor cursed:
The Heracles-anger that burned in his heart went
  straight for the biggest and worst.

Through a terrible stench of hides he strode, through
threats of murder and mud,
And faced in battle the Beast himself, the jag-toothed
shedder of blood,
Whose eyes flashed fire in his lordly ire, like a whore
beginning to swear,
And a hundred damned blackmailers' tongues came
flickering out of his hair:
A voice like a torrent, begetter of death, as it bursts in
a flood without trammel,
The smell of a seal, the groin of a witch—unwashed—
and the rump of a camel. (*Peace*, 751–8)

In the *Wasps* he had continued an almost identical passage with some lines about informers:

He looked that Monstrosity straight in the face, he
recked not of favour nor fear,
But fought your cause as he fights it to-day; and after-
wards, only last year,
He turned his hand to the scum that remained,[1] the
Fevers and Shivering-Fits
Who choked your fathers at night, and drove your
grandfathers out of their wits;
Who coiled themselves up in the dark on the beds of
the quietest people, with strings
Of charges, sub-poenas, injunctions and writs, till up
leapt the poor old things
And ran to the Polemarch screaming for help, whole
troops of them, straight out of bed! (*Wasps* 1036 ff.)

[1] In the *Holkades* (*Merchant Ships*), produced at the Lenaea, 423 B.C.,
he attacked Cleon's satellites; Kock suggests that the Athenians and
Spartans, wishing to state their grievances against each other, found
that the grievances could only be carried in heavy freight vessels, and
that one load was as heavy and disgusting as the other! Thereupon they
made peace.—This suits the fragments.

The Polemarch was the official appointed to look after the interests of non-citizens. The informers and professional spy-hunters doubtless found their favourite victims among the islanders and other resident aliens, especially among the old and quiet and well-to-do, who had never seen the inside of a law-court, and could most easily be browbeaten and plundered.

These passages are worth thinking over. They serve to show the mistakenness of the common view that all the comic writers were much the same: that they all exercised their personal quarrels, that they were all, as satirists, 'agin' the government', and that Aristophanes merely ran with his pack. It seems true, in the first place, that he did not turn his satire against 'women and poor little private men'. Some of the attacks of Cratînus and Eupolis on Pericles were violently insulting towards Aspasia. Hermippus wrote his *Breadsellers* and Eupolis his *Maricâs* definitely on Hyperbolus and his mother—represented as a drunken old woman 'with a dance'. Plato Comicus wrote a play on Autolycus, a notoriously handsome youth; another on the flatterers of the rich and profligate Callias—neither of them political leaders. Aristophanes seems to have kept his hands clean from this sort of thing. He did not even use his heavy artillery on the lesser lights of politics, as Plato did in his *Cleophon*, and *Pisander*, and *Alliance*— which dealt with the ostracism of Hyperbolus.

In championing the oppressed Allies, again, he seems to have stood almost solitary. He claims that he alone had 'dared to tell the Athenians the truth to their faces'. Tourists came from abroad specially to see such a curiosity among poets! (*Ach.* 642 ff.) True, Eupolis co-operated with him in the *Knights*, and wrote *The Cities*—in which the Allied Cities, as slaves, were shown appealing to the Courts to be sold to a kinder master. But Eupolis broke with Aristophanes, and no one else seems to have stepped into the breach. Plato Comicus in his *Hellas*, or *The Islands*, was imperialist; and even Eupolis complained of the public interest in poets who were not true Athenians.

Nor was the cause of Peace by any means specially popular among the comic writers. Probably on the whole they were against the democratic war party as the litterati generally were, and their constant attacks on Hyperbolus and Cleophon must have implied some advocacy of peace rather than war. But peace is not prominent in the fragments. Pericles is attacked for his Olympian or dictatorial position, for the size and shape of his head, and the like, not for his war policy; more than once also, as Hermippus puts it, for his policy of avoiding battle and only 'gnashing his teeth when bitten by a red-hot . . . Cleon'.[1] Hyperbolus and

---

[1] Cratînus, *Thrâttae, Nemesis, Chirones*; Teleclîdes, 42; Hermippus, 46. Cf. Thuc. II. 21, 59.

Cleophon are attacked for their vulgarity; for their
bad choice in the matter of mothers; for the spy-
mania which they throve upon; and Hyperbolus
at any rate for his bad pronunciation. He said
Ἀητώμην, ὀλίον instead of Ἀιητώμην and ὀλίγον, which
seems to have been a vulgar weakness, not an
aristocratic one like Alcibiades' lisp. (Plato, fr.
168; *Wasps*, 44.)

Aristophanes was a good hater, and did his
hating in a good and generous cause. However,
at the time of the *Peace*, though the old feud
against Cleon and his gang of 'patriots' is not
forgotten, for the most part the poet has laid aside
his domestic grievances as well as his anger against
the enemy, and, with the majority for once on his
side, contents himself with singing a paean of
reconciliation.[1]

---

[1] There was a *Second Peace* in the official lists, but ancient scholars
did not know whether it was a different play (e.g. was the *Georgoi* also
called *Peace?*) or a revised version. There was also a *Second Thesmophoriazusae* (or Θεσμοφοριάσασαι), which depicted the last day of the
Festival, when the fast was over: Kock gives 28 fragments. Our *Plutus*
is the *Second Plutus*, the first having been played 'twenty years earlier'
(*Schol. Plut.* 183). The other cases are different, the *Frogs* being
encored because of its success, the *Clouds* rewritten because of its
failure.

CHAPTER III

THE JURY COURTS
(*Wasps*)

THERE was in Athens another well-spring of continuous trouble against which Aristophanes made public protest. The Dicastêria, or Law-courts, were organized on a highly democratic system, yet one which in normal circumstances effectively prevented corruption and intimidation and gave considerable guarantees against injustice.[1] The qualified citizens were divided into ten bodies of 'Dicastae' with full powers of both verdict and sentence; each 'jury' had to consist of 500 citizens. They tried both civil and criminal cases; in some instances the State provided a public prosecutor while the prisoner had his advocate or advocates. Bribery of five hundred individuals would in any case be difficult, and it was made much more so by a peculiar rule: it was not settled till the last moment which cases would come before which jury. Even so, no doubt, a really corrupt society could have got round the regulations, and it is a sign of the general soundness of Athenian public life that we scarcely ever hear of any attempt to corrupt the jury courts.

But a system that works in normal circumstances may easily break down in times of revolution,

[1] See especially, on the comparative immunity of Athens from intimidation, Grote's *History*, v, pp. 237 ff.

poverty, or war. War made the Athenian madly
suspicious. The French Revolution and the World
War show abundant instances of the hold which
suspicion-mania can obtain over a population which
has once begun to brood upon 'hidden hands'.
Again, it must be remembered that at this time
the citizens of military age were mostly away on
active service: the Courts were manned by the old
men who could no longer fight and were probably
more bitter in consequence. Then the class war
between rich and poor, which so largely underlay
the war between Sparta and Athens, introduced a
further element of savage prejudice. And the
pressure of poverty, and sometimes of actual
famine, on the Athenian people made all trials for
offences which involved confiscation into terrible
temptations. We remember in the *Knights* the
question addressed to Demos. 'If some disrepu-
table public prosecutor says to the Court, "There
is no bread for you jurymen unless you condemn
the prisoner", what will you say?' In the later
years of the war Lysias, when prosecuting some
false accusers, says, 'You have often heard these
people, when they wanted to ruin a prisoner, explain that unless you give the verdict they wish the
jury-pay will fail' (27. 1). Again he remarks that
the Boulê, when it has enough funds to carry on,
is scrupulously just; but when it falls into need it
is compelled to admit impeachments and confiscations of property, and to follow the most unprin-

cipled proposals that speakers make. We have seen
in the *Knights* how Cleon brazenly defended such
confiscations, using exactly the same arguments as
the leaders of the French Revolution.

There never was in Athens the same ferocity or
wholesale bloodshed as in that Revolution; but
parallels from the nearer and perhaps more barbarous time may illustrate the troubles of the
ancient civilization, about which we have fewer
details. There never was in Athens, as there was
in Paris, a Tribunal which tried prisoners in
batches of sixty, was relieved of the laws of evidence, and gave no sentence but death. But the
Athenian *sycophantai*, against whom Aristophanes
is always fighting, become more intelligible when
we observe some of the minor agents of the Terror.
A madman like Héron, for example, who suspects
every one and quarrels with every one, becomes
an agent of the Comité de Sûreté Générale and has
a band of men, 'porteurs d'ordre', who 'rabattent
du gibier pour la guillotine', including most of
Héron's personal enemies and incidentally his wife
(*Vieilles Maisons, Vieux Papiers*, i. 68 ff.). A certain Dossonville, again, saves himself from danger
by getting into the police, and obtains special
powers. He can detain and examine in prison
without witnesses any person he pleases. He has a
pass from the Government declaring that he
'must not be arrested or interrupted or imprisoned
on any pretext whatever'. Common thieves, like

the Englishman Grieve, made large sums by black-mailing rich persons as long as they had any money left, and when that failed denouncing them, as Grieve did with Mme du Barry (ii. 110). By a somewhat more refined or elaborate villainy, Dr. Belhomme obtained from some influential person a promise that the inmates of his Maison de Santé should not be arrested. He was thus enabled to charge fabulous sums for pension, and when the Duchesse du Châtelet at last refused to pay and left him, he was able to point to her immediate execution as the 'result of misplaced economy' (iii. 130 ff.). The French juries were not unmanageably large like the Athenian; but the attendance of turbulent crowds introduced a much more dangerous element of mob passion into the administration of law than the large numbers of the Athenian dicasts.

The *Wasps* was produced in January or February 422 B.C., at the Lenaea, but unfortunately the extract from the official record, or Didascalia, has come down to us in a corrupt state. We cannot be sure whether it won the first or the second prize, nor whether Aristophanes produced the play in his own name or in that of Philônides, like the *Clouds* and the *Frogs*. On the whole I am disposed to accept Mr. Rogers's treatment of the text:

It received first prize: Philônides with the *Rehearsal* second, Leucon with the *Ambassadors* third.

The *Rehearsal*, which seems to have been a parody of some tragedy on the Thyestes story, is always elsewhere treated as the work Aristophanes himself. Thus it looks as if, on this one occasion, Aristophanes had actually two plays in the competition, the *Wasps* under his own name, and the *Rehearsal* under that of Philônides.

It was, as we have noticed, a time of poverty, and the old men, past military age, cut off from their farms in the country and unable to find ordinary employment, were dependent on the fee of three obols which they got for attendance at the Court. They come in the dark before dawn to summon their friend Philocleon. It is to be a great day. The general Lachês, rich and simple-minded, is up for trial, and a 'fat' man from Thrace as well. The two should make up for the disappointment of yesterday when a man from Samos escaped by proving that he had not been in the conspiracy, but on the contrary—confound him!—had detected and betrayed the conspirators. The old men move along in good spirits, with the old-world music of Phrynichus on their lips, but they are desperately hard up. The lamps they carry scarcely burn, but when their boys pull the wick higher the father beats them. Oil is so dear nowadays! When the children beg for some figs the old men frankly lose their tempers. 'Figs, indeed! No!' 'If by chance the Court should not sit to-day, will there be no breakfast at all?' ask the children; 'No, nor dinner either.' And the children cry. (See 240 ff., 280–315.)

But let us take the plot of the play. Old Philocleon (*Love-Cleon*), the juryman, has gone mad
with love of judging. His son, Bdelycleon (*Loathe-
Cleon*), has tried various cures upon him and at last
has imprisoned him in his house. His fellow
dicasts, fierce old men with stings like wasps, come
to fetch him to Court, and soon there is the inevitable Agôn. The father maintains that a dicast's
life is the most glorious in the world, with everybody flattering and fearing him, and the famous
orators swearing, 'O People, I will never betray
you!'

The son begins his answer with an apology. It
is a difficult job, and altogether too big for a
mere comedian, to cure an inveterate disease in
the heart of the State. Then he plunges into a
question of finance. Take first the tribute from
the Allied Cities; then the taxes and 'the various
one-per-cents', court-fees, mine-rents, market and
harbour dues, rents and confiscations: the total
cannot be much less than 2,000 talents. (In gold,
about half a million pounds.) 'How much of that
do *you* get? Take as the very maximum, 6,000
dicasts, sitting 300 days in the year at 3 obols a
day, it would only come to 150 talents—less than
one-tenth of the whole. Where does all the rest
go? Inquire of your orators and "never-betrayers",
who are now telling you that you cannot get
enough to eat unless the tribute of the Allies is
increased. Ask them to steal less or to give you

some share in the prizes and cushy jobs and graft. Or ask the Allied Cities to undertake the support of twenty Athenians each; they will do it gladly and feed you like princes!'

Aristophanes is still championing the Allied Cities. The original tribute, fixed by Aristides, came to about 450 talents, but three years before the production of the *Wasps* it had been nearly trebled. It was now about 1,300 talents, and there was talk of increasing it again. 'Squeeze the Allies still harder', argued the war-party, 'or else there will not be enough to feed the people!' 'Rubbish!' says Aristophanes. 'Feeding the people is a trifle. It is your wretched war and your rapacious ways of collecting revenue that use up all the funds.' At least that is what he would say if he were perfectly serious. For his present purpose he is content to show merely that the hungry Demos, whom the orators are professing such anxiety to feed, receives less than a tenth of the sums collected.

The Wasps listen and are convinced. They see that they have been made fools of. But old Philocleon is harder to move. He cannot live without his one pleasure. He *must* try cases and judge and vote. Very good, says his son; but why should he not conduct his trials at home, in comfort, at such times as suit himself? He consents to make the experiment and—by a fortunate coincidence—his dog Labês, a native of the deme Aixônê, is suspected of having stolen some Sicilian cheese, while a dog from Kudathênaion is brought forward to accuse him. Lachês of Aixônê, the brave and simple soldier who is known to us by Plato's Dialogue *Laches*, had recently been prosecuted by Cleon of Kudathênaion for some incident in his Sicilian campaign, and the mock trial evidently contains some references to the real one. Lachês, we remember, was 'up for trial to-day' (240).

The dog Labês is unable to speak, being paralysed by the shock of the surroundings, as old Thucydides, the much respected leader of the Moderates, was at his famous trial, and as very likely Lachês himself may have been. The accusing dog can, and does, at least utter loud 'Bow-wows', though for the actual speech he uses an advocate. The slave Sôsias speaks for him, and is made to use the rough platform metaphors which we know to have been characteristic of Cleon. The prisoner has done awful things to 'me and the yo-heave-hoes'—τὸ ῥυππαπαί—meaning the democratic sailor population; he got away in a corner and 'Sicilized' his booty—just the sort of word a demagogue would coin to suggest that the generals far away in Sicily were up to mischief. The prisoner is 'the lone-eatingest of dogs'—μονοφαγί-στατος—which is hardly a natural expression. The whole passage reminds one of the parody of Cleon's language in the *Knights*, 461 ff.[1]

[1] Cleon there sees plots being τεκταινόμενα, γομφούμενα, κολλώμενα (carpentered, pegged, and glued), and the Offal-monger retorts by seeing

Philocleon bullies the prisoner like a Judge
Jeffreys and is affected by no arguments. Bdelycleon, as counsel for the defence, does his best.
The poor dog has never been taught to play the
harp, so no wonder he has got into difficulties—
a hit, it would seem, at the uncultured Lachês. But
he is a good dog. He fights your enemies. He
hunts the wolves. He lives on scraps and refuse.
His messmates—the pot, pestle, and water-jug—
all speak well of him. He runs everywhere, while
his accuser simply stays at home and bites every-
one who possesses anything and won't give him
half! Philocleon is slightly moved, and the production of the prisoner's wife and weeping puppies
at the critical moment is just too much for him:
'Enough!' he cries, 'Get down, get down!' (κατάβα,
κατάβα, κατάβα, κατάβα). The defence think their
case is won, but the old Dicast soon masters his
unworthy weakness and goes to put his vote in the
first of the two urns, which means Guilty. By
some trick of his son's, which we cannot now trace
out, the first urn is concealed from him, so that he
thinks the second is the first, and unintentionally
acquits the prisoner. On learning the result he
faints. Never has he let a prisoner off before.
May the Gods forgive him! An oracle had
warned him of old that if ever such a disaster

others συμφυσώμενα and χαλκευόμενα. Mr. Denniston has pointed out in an
interesting paper, *C.Q.* xxi. 34 (June 1927), many unsuspected instances
of this kind of parody in Aristophanes.

occurred he would waste away and die! (994–7, cf. 160).

The end of the play is a surprise. Bdelycleon promises to look after his father; to take him into society, to dinners, suppers, and public sights, and make him happy. Meantime he must improve his dress and his manners.

After the parabasis we find the old man in violent protest against all this coddling. He hates his warm new Persian cloak, his smart Laconian shoes. He *likes* to be cold. He *likes* chilblains. However, he submits, and is then instructed in the arts of polite (or snobbish?) conversation. Can he tell stories? . . . He can, but they prove to be quite the wrong sort. He ought to relate how once he was on an Official Mission with So-and-so and So-and-So; how he was present at a famous contest at Olympia; how he distinguished himself at a wild-boar hunt or the like. Then he is made·to imagine himself at a fashionable dinner party, and taught to recline properly at table, to wash his hands, to pour the libation, to sing a *Scolion* worthy of the highly distinguished company he is supposed to be meeting—such as Theôrus the 'god-forsaken', the poverty-stricken Aeschines, the barbarous Akestor, and the unspeakable Cleon himself. Philocleon at first demurs to the idea of a wine-party. Drink always makes him noisy and ends in the police court. It is explained to him, however, that men of fashion can always carry their wine, or, if they do make some error, they can put it right without delay by a witty apology, and are never fined or imprisoned. That being so, he consents and goes off to the party.

In the next scene we see the result of this teaching. Old Philocleon has been to the party and more than enjoyed himself. He has beaten the slaves, insulted all his fellow guests, and carried off the flute-girl who was entertaining them. He has even promised to make her his mistress and give her plenty of money as soon as his son, who keeps him devilish close, is dead! He is pursued by various people whom he has beaten or mocked at in the streets, and gets the better of all of them by high spirits and impudence, and drunken attempts to tell witty stories, till his son has to carry him off into the house. In a few moments, however, the deplorable old gentleman is out again and proceeds to dance the chorus off the orchestra in a *cordax*.

It is wild farce, but we have learnt to see the serious issues that underlie the farce of Aristophanes. We have already noticed the poverty of the Old Men who act as Dicasts and the ominous fact that the prisoners whom they are trying are rich. Confiscations are one way, and sometimes perhaps the only way, of making two ends meet. The play is full of references to the συκοφάνται, however we translate the word: 'informers', or 'professional accusers', or 'blackmailers'. We hear

also of κόλακες, 'flatterers' or 'toadies', though it is
not perfectly clear whom they flatter. They flatter
the Demos, of course, as we were told in the
Knights: they swear that they love the common
people and will never be false to them (666 ff.).
They also toady Cleon and his kind, the men of
the hour. The god-forsaken and perjured Theôrus
is one of them (45, 47, 418, *Cl.* 400); another the
gross Cleônymus, who lives by prosecutions and
who once threw away his shield (592). Listening to
these people, we are told, the Demos is like a herd
of huddled sheep. One character has a dream in
which he sees a great mass of sheep sitting in the
ecclesia, being addressed by a great sea-monster
with a voice like that of a pig being singed, and
smelling—we are not surprised to hear—of a
tannery (31 ff.). We can guess the sort of accusations that go down with these sheep. Charges of
conspiracies against the people, or just conspiracies
in general, not further defined (288, 345). 'You
are an enemy of the people', say the Chorus to
Bdelycleon. 'You are a monarchist, you associate
with Brasidas; you wear a border to your cloak,
you scoundrel; you keep an unshaven lip!' (474–
6). (The last two crimes are ways of imitating the
Spartans.) But the favourite charge, apparently,
is a charge of attempting to overthrow the constitution and set up a Tyranny. 'Everything with
you', says Bdelycleon, 'is tyranny and conspirators;
I had never so much as heard the name of such a

thing for fifty years, and now it is commoner than red herrings!' (487–99).

Through the light jests one feels Aristophanes' horror at the sheer ferocity of the Courts. Old Philocleon never cares for a prisoner's prayers: 'You are trying to boil a stone', he would say, if they thought to melt his heart. He knows he is feared: 'You yourself fear me', he says to his son, 'but I am damned if I fear you!' (νὴ τὴν Δήμητρα, Δέδοικας. ἐγὼ Δ' ἀπολοίμην εἴ σε Δέδοικα, 629–30). There is something horrible in his appeal to Lykos —the name means Wolf—the hero whose statue stood near the Dicastêrion, where the jury received their pay: 'Hail, O hero Lykos, my master and neighbour; you take your pleasure, just as I do, in the tears and lamentations of prisoners in the dock. That is why you come and live on purpose where you can hear them—the only immortal who sits beside those who weep!' (389 ff.). Almost equally repulsive is Philocleon's account of the glory of the Dicast's life. How great tall men, who would otherwise never have known him, come fawning upon him and praying for his goodwill; how he lets himself be coaxed, and then forgets his promise and sits listening, as if to a play, while they utter every note they can think of, that may help them to escape. The wits make jokes to please him. The artists perform, the actors recite, and the musicians play, in the hope of winning his favour. Prisoners bring forward their wives and children and their pretty daughters, and they all bow their heads and bleat together in the hope of moving him. And he just enjoys the show! (ἐγὼ Δ' ἀκροῶμαι). Nay, he plays with the laws and sets aside wills, if he pleases, and disinherits heiresses. And the greatest men in the State, Euathlos, and the great fat Flatterônymos,[1] the Shield-dropper, and Theôrus and Cleon himself fan him and brush his boots and whisper how they love him! (550–600).

It is a horrible picture. One feels a chivalrous indignation behind the laughter. Yet, the curious thing is that Philocleon and his waspish colleagues are treated with a kind of personal sympathy. It is not war to the knife against them, as it is against Cleon and the Kolakes. The truth is that the juries were largely composed of just the class of men that Aristophanes liked and championed: the old men from the country, prevented by the war from attending to their farms, prevented by their age from going on military expeditions—military service normally ceased at 60—and consequently left in Athens, old, respectable, very poor, embittered and angry, able to serve on juries or sit in the ecclesia, and—according to Aristophanes— offering an easy prey to any smart and unscrupulous speaker who chose to gull them. They are like the old charcoal-burners of the *Acharnians*; they too were 'Marathônomachai', the type that

---

[1] Κολακώνυμος ἀσπιΔαποβλής, i.e. a mixture of Cleonymos and κόλαξ, a flatterer.

had fought sixty-five years before at Marathon, and, fierce and narrow as they might be, their hearts were in the right place. Bdelycleon's case against them is that they are deceived. 'Who gets the enormous revenues of the state?—not you the Dicasts. Who gets the presents and lawyers' fees from the Allied Cities? Not you. Who gets the fees offered by the prisoners? The smart lawyers and politicians, the flatterers and humbugs who are always vowing their devotion to you. They lie to you all the time, and make you condemn the innocent!' The Dicasts are tough old veterans, men of a harder and honester age. Wasps, he calls them; true Attic wasps, for all who have troubled their nest have felt their stings. When the barbarian came to smoke them out, they stuck together man by man, bit their lower lips, and stood fast while the sun was hidden by the enemy's arrows (1075–90).

The poet strikes a sympathetic note right at their entrance. One cannot but like these vigorous Old Warriors who are up before dawn to do their public service,

> Lights in their hands, old music on their lips,
> Wild honey and the East and Phrynichus.

Phrynichus belonged to the Marathon time, or even earlier, the time when Athens was a city of heroes. Later on they go even farther back than Phrynichus, to the songs of Thespis (217–20, 269, 1479). Men were rough and simple then. They did not understand modern refinement and despised modern luxuries. This is, I think, the clue to the end of the play. The old Marathon-warrior, if left to himself, is content with his old threadbare coat, his bare feet, and his chilblains. He does not want to go into smart society. As for a drinking-party, he prefers to keep out of it, and stay quiet. But if by chance he does drink . . . well, people of this degenerate age had better look out!

CHAPTER IV

THE NEW LEARNING: SOCRATES
(*Clouds*)

THE *Clouds* can be regarded as a development of the *Daitalês*, much as the *Knights* and the *Wasps* are developments of the *Babylonians*. Aristophanes' indignation at the general oppression of the islands by Athens leads up to an attack on the prime author of the oppression, Cleon, and a study of his half-innocent instruments, the Dicastae. So the contrast between the two current forms of moral and intellectual training, the old and the new, the country and the city, led on to a study of the greatest representative of the new culture, both moral and intellectual, and the 'clash of humours' to which his activity gave rise.

A whole library of controversy has gathered about the *Clouds*. For one thing, it deals with one of the most interesting figures of antiquity, Socrates, and adds to the two intimate and discrepant accounts which we possess in Plato and Xenophon, a third equally intimate and discrepant in a different way. For another, we know that the play was not successful, though the author thought it the cleverest thing he had written, and that he rewrote it in its present form for a second performance, which apparently did not take place—at least, not at the official festival. Lastly, there is the difficulty

inseparable from comedy, especially when the
comedy is two thousand five hundred years old,
that we cannot be quite sure of detecting every joke
that is present, or, when we have detected its presence, of seeing precisely what it is. For example,
if the scholars of A.D. 2500 were to discover some
present-day farce in which a man from Aberdeen
was represented as wildly scattering his money, or
Dr. Einstein as refusing to pay his year's rent on
the ground that Time does not exist, or the Curate
in the Bab Ballads as having a theatrical fairy for
his mother, how could they know, without corro-
borative evidence, that the first joke was meant to
be the opposite of the truth, the second a caricature of the truth, while the third had no relation
to the truth at all? Might we not easily have a
scholiast explaining that Aberdonians were notorious spendthrifts, that Dr. Einstein was accused
of not paying his debts, and that the Church of
England was sadly tainted with profligacy?

Let us try, at least, to clear away some of the
preliminary problems. What made the play fail,
and what was Aristophanes aiming at in his 'second
edition'? He tells us in the parabasis. The play
was too 'high-brow'. He thought it the cleverest
(σοφώτατ' ἔχειν) of his comedies; he had expected
an audience consisting of men of taste (Δεξιοί);
he had taken great pains over the work; and he
had been beaten by vulgar fellows, by regular
'low-brows' (ὑπ' ἀνΔρῶν φορτικῶν) who relied on

scurrility and horse-play. Nevertheless he will 'not betray the men of taste who believe in him' (520-7).

This parabasis obviously forms part of the second edition. We can even to some extent date it, since it refers to the *Maricâs* of Eupolis, which was produced in 421 B.C., but it does not know of the ostracism of Hyperbolus in 417 B.C. Besides the parabasis we know from the scholia of two particular scenes which 'were substituted' in the second edition; a debate between the Just Cause and Unjust Cause (Δίκαιος καὶ Ἄδικος Λόγος) and the final scene, in which Socrates and his disciples are burnt out of their house like vermin.[1] Now these are the chief, and we may say the only, places where there is anything like a denunciation of Socrates as a wicked influence. The rest of the play is quite different in tone; it is 'humour' in the Elizabethan sense, not denunciation. If we now look back to the parabasis we shall see that he appeals to the audience to look with favour on this play as they had on the 'good young man and the corrupt young man' in the *Daitalês* (529).

This seems to me to show that the first edition of the *Clouds* was too subtle for the public, that it treated Socrates and his school too sympathetically

[1] Hypothesis VI. ἡ μὲν παράβασις τοῦ χοροῦ ἥμειπται, καὶ ὅπου ὁ Δίκαιος Λόγος πρὸς τὸν Ἄδικον λαλεῖ, καὶ τελευταῖον ὅπου καίεται ἡ Διατριβὴ Σωκράτους. I cannot think, with Mr. Rogers, that the second phrase, 'where the Just Cause talks with the Unjust', means only the speech of the Just Cause.

and with too much friendly humour instead of rough satire; that this caused, or was supposed to have caused, the failure of the play, and that Aristophanes in self-defence tried to explain that of course he was against the new learning altogether, just as he had been in the *Daitalês*. To make this clearer, he inserted in the second version the debate between the Just and Unjust Causes, and the burning of Socrates' house. The play in its revised form was widely read, and may no doubt have been performed unofficially, though it never actually was awarded a Chorus. It is often referred to by later writers, and it seems to have played its part in the tragedy of 399, where, according to Plato, the attacks of the comic poets formed one powerful element among the causes that led to the judicial murder of Socrates (*Apol.* 18 b, 19 c).

The plot gives us, as usual, an elderly farmer for hero, but not of the usual shrewd and honest type like Dicaiopolis. Strepsiades ('Twister') is a bit of a fool and far from honest. He has married a rich fashionable wife and has been ruined by her debts and those of his smart and horse-loving son, Pheidippides. Almost in despair, he recollects that there is in Athens a frightfully clever man called Socrates who can for a small fee make the Worse Cause appear the Better and will be able to teach him how to defraud his creditors. He begs Pheidippides to become a disciple of the philosopher, who (so he has heard) is surrounded by a circle of

the smartest young aristocrats, the καλοὶ κἀγαθοί.
That is the rumour, but Pheidippides knows better.
He has seen Socrates surrounded by his pale half-
starved disciples, and refuses the proposal with disgust. The old Strepsiades has no choice but to go
to the Phrontistêrion—the Thinking Laboratory
or 'Thinkery'—himself. Socrates accepts him—
it should be noticed—without mentioning fees at
all, but merely insisting on the need of hard work
and unluxurious living, and introduces him to the
Clouds, who are the deities and patrons of his sect.
It is they, not Zeus, who cause rain; they who
cause thunder and lightning. The Clouds accept
the new pupil on conditions:

O mortal athirst for the Wisdom High, which only the
    Clouds can give,
How blest in Athens your state shall be, and wherever
    Greek men live,
If you ponder well, and remember well, and in heart
    are patient and bold,
And can stand for ever, and walk for ever, nor care one
    jot for the cold,
If you never essay two meals in a day, and abstain from
    the drinking of wine,
And 'gyms' and follies, and make up your mind, like
    a man of intelligence fine,
To be never defeated in practical life, nor in thought,
    nor war of the word.

A more imaginative man might have shrunk
from this severe programme, but, as far as mere
hardship goes, the Twister is not frightened. They

can hammer him on an anvil if they like. Nor does he
object to the second condition, that he must recognize the gods worshipped by the philosophers, and
only those. 'Good; he won't so much as speak to
the others if he meets them in the street.' On his
side he only wants to be the best speaker in Greece
by a hundred stades, and thus be able to elude his
creditors. Socrates has left the conversation before
this, and the Clouds—somewhat grimly—promise
that he shall get what he desires.

He enters the school and is deprived of such
superfluous comforts as shoes and cloak. Socrates
tries to teach him the elements of 'wisdom'—a
little science, metre, and grammar—but finds him
impossibly stupid. He cannot see the good of all
this irrelevant learning. He just wants to be taught
how to cheat his creditors, not anything else.
Finally Socrates, in the true spirit of the Socratic
education, leaves him wrapped in a blanket to
think an original thought by himself. Strepsiades
thinks only of his debts; Socrates in vain urges him
to let his mind move freely away from himself and
mix with the circumambient atmosphere. It is no
use; he can think of nothing but himself and
his debts, and he forgets everything he is told.
Socrates at last expels him, and the Leader of the
Clouds suggests that he might send his son in his
place. Reluctantly and contemptuously Pheidippides consents, and Socrates—by a rather abrupt
turn—hands him over to be educated by the Two

Words, or Causes, Just and Unjust. There is a contest or battle of words between them. The Just
Cause pleads for the old simple chaste life, the
Unjust for a completely sceptical philosophy and
a do-as-you-please morality. He points to the
success of the worst scallywags in all branches of
life, till, at the end of the Agôn, the Just Cause is
not only defeated but converted, and jumps over
to join the scallywags himself! Pheidippides is
taken into the school, and in due course is certified
as fully trained. He instructs his father in a few
sophisms. The old man plays these off with enthusiasm on two creditors who come for payment,
and then goes in triumphantly to rejoin his son at
a feast. Presently he comes out crying for help:
'O for the hide of a tortoise!' He had a difference
of opinion with Pheidippides at dinner and rebuked
him for singing a shocking song of Euripides about
the love of a brother for a sister, whereupon Pheidippides actually beat him! Pheidippides follows
and proves that it is simple justice that he should
beat his father for his good, as years ago his father
had beaten him for his good. To make justice perfect, however, he promises to beat his mother too.

Strepsiades appeals to the Clouds for help or
mercy. They, in answer, show him that it has all
been his own fault. They saw at the time the
wickedness of his desires and allowed him to destroy
himself. He tries to reason with Pheidippides,
who remains true to his new heroes and believes

in neither the gods nor the laws. He then asks counsel of the Hermes who stands before the house, and by his advice, rushes, together with his slaves, to burn out the whole hornet's nest of Socrates and the disciples.

Now the most generally accepted view of this play, from Grote onwards, is to regard it as a general attack on the sophistic movement or 'new learning', with Socrates, the most eminent Athenian philosopher of the time, cast quite unjustly and with no regard to truth for the part of the typical sophist. The typical sophist is supposed to have been a mixture of the quack savant and the unscrupulous popular orator, and the Socrates of the *Clouds* to stand vaguely for both, while the real Socrates was not at all like either. This view has, to my mind, been disproved or at least very drastically corrected by Professor Taylor in *Varia Socratica*. The Socrates of the *Clouds*, he argues, is not in the least like an unscrupulous and rapacious orator, not yet like a rich fashionable sophist, such as Hippias or Protagoras; while on the other hand he does in a number of detailed points closely resemble the real Socrates.

He is the centre of a school or body of intimates whom Plato calls φιλόσοφοι and Aristophanes φροντισταί. They had a common table (*Cl.* 175), they lived, as Plato says, 'in extreme poverty', with no cloak, no shoes, and the barest sort of bed (*Cl.* 834–8, 412–19, 498, 719), enduring hunger and

cold without complaint. The 'thinkers', as Eupolis
also said (fr. 352), have 'thought out every problem except how to get enough to eat'. They
studied physics, inquired how many of its own
feet a flea could jump, how a gnat made its noise,
what was the cause of rain and what of thunder;
they had maps and astronomical plans, and so on.
In later life, it is true, Socrates had given up these
studies, but he tells us in the *Phaedo* (96 a–e) how
passionately he pursued them in his youth. The
'thinkers' laid stress on Ἀήρ, thick air or mist, and
the circular movement (Δῖνος) of the sky, as a
cause of those thin material objects which we call
'spiritual' (264, 329–30), which gives Aristophanes the chance of making them worshippers
of the Clouds. They probably did not accept the
Gods of the City in their ordinary mythological
form, though they were much occupied with religion and the after life. Hence the charge against
Socrates at his trial that he did not accept the City's
Gods, but other strange gods (cf. *Cl.* 247, 380, 1471,
423–4, 817–19, Ὁ Μήλιος 830). These are general
characteristics, but we hear something also of the
Master's personal mannerisms, the deep reveries
on divine or eternal subjects from which 'creatures
of a day' could scarcely rouse him by the loudest
shouting (218–25): how he ἐβρενθύετο ἐν ταῖσιν
ὁδοῖς (362) and paid little attention to the common world about him; how he looked sideways
from under his brows in the way that Plato

describes (*Phaedo*, 117 b; *Cl.* 362 f.), how he walked barefoot, and perhaps how he objected to music at meals. (Cf. *Protag.* 347 c, d with *Cl.* 1357 ff.) We hear of his theory of thoughts born from a soul in labour by the help of μαιευτική or 'midwifery' (137); we see him trying to get his pupil to think for himself (695 ff.), and laying special stress on the importance of memory, as Socrates did on ἀνάμνησις. We hear of the crowds who flocked to consult this strange being (469), and—strangest of all—we hear of the καλοὶ κἀγαθοί, or young aristocrats of fashion, who frequent his society. We even see one of them reluctantly taking his school and taking it, as no doubt they often did, in the wrong spirit.

The likeness to Socrates, and indeed the direct imitation of various characteristics of Socrates, are to my mind unmistakable. But can we fairly call the piece, as a whole, a satire or attack on Socrates?[1] There is no attack on his honour. He is not represented as charging high fees—the joke about Hyperbolus in 876 cannot have much to do with Socrates—, as catering for rich pupils, or as professing magical powers which he does not possess. His morals, in the narrower sense, are left absolutely unassailed. Even his disciples, apart from the charges of being dirty and unkempt, which

---

[1] A similar question will arise later about the poet's attitude to Euripides: see Chapter V. The two were associated in men's minds: 'Socrates supplied the sticks' when Euripides lit a fire. Teleclîdes, fr. 40.

was merely one side of their asceticism, get off with the mild condemnation of being 'idle' and 'chatterers'. Of course, strictly speaking, Socrates should—and would—never have taken a pupil who only wanted 'wisdom' in order to learn how not to pay his debts, but that is, so to speak, a necessary part of the plot, and though Aristophanes does not take the trouble to represent Strepsiades as concealing his nefarious purpose from the Master, he never represents Socrates as teaching him how to achieve it.

The joke of the play, so to speak, is not any suggested roguery of Socrates, but a much subtler and more amusing joke: the clash of 'humours' when a stupid dishonest old 'low-brow', like Strepsiades, is brought into the school of ascetic contemplative students with their minds set on mathematics and τὰ μετέωρα and things not of this world. The Twister is not a shrewd rustic like Dicaiopolis or Trygaios; he is for the most part not the mocker but the butt.

He misunderstands everything he is taught, and misunderstands it in a 'low-brow' manner: the physical experiments, the map, the 'measuring of land'. When he hears that the αἰθέριος Δῖνος, or revolution of the sky, causes movements of the clouds, he thinks Dinos is a person. He can remember what is owed to him, but forgets what he owes. He 'cannot speak, but he can cheat' (483–96). He is helpless about metre and grammar;

still more helpless when set to contemplate and produce an original thought. The thought he produces is only a way of cheating. As Socrates says, he can never get his thoughts away from himself (761). All learning and philosophy is for him a way of making money or at least not paying it. 'What good would my learning be to me if I paid?' (1231, 1250).

It is true that Aristophanes mocks at learning, in the regular style of ancient comedy, as well as at ignorance. He complains of Metôn's attempt to improve the Calendar (610–26), and in the last scene professes to treat astronomy as an impious attempt to pry into the privacy of the gods (1506 ff.). And no doubt some of Strepsiades' stupidities are jokes of double edge, cutting the learned doctor as well as the half-idiotic pupil; but in the main the laughter is against the Twister, not for him. The whole makes on me the impression not of a satire, like the *Knights* or the *Wasps*, directed against something the poet hated and wanted to destroy, but of a 'clash of humours'.

A Doctor of Letters of my acquaintance once received a letter from a West African negro, stating in respectful terms that he had been informed that the learned man possessed a pill which enabled people to pass examinations, particularly in arithmetic and English grammar, and asking the price of it, since he wanted a post in the Government service. Imagine a farce in which the African came to be instructed by Professor Eddington; the professor tried to teach him mathematics or physics or astronomy, and the pupil kept wondering when the pill was coming: that would give the sort of 'clash of humours' that I mean, but it would not necessarily be an attack on Professor Eddington.

There are two other points which must be in our minds if we mean to form any adequate conception of the purpose of the *Clouds* and the feelings of Aristophanes towards Socrates. One is a confirmation of the line we have taken above: Aristophanes was a personal friend of Socrates, and is introduced by Plato as one of the important speakers in that select and ever-famous wine-party immortalized in the *Symposium*. The other may cause a moment's difficulty. According to Plato, when Socrates stood upon his trial, twenty-four years after the *Clouds*, he felt his most serious danger to be the general misunderstanding and prejudice caused in the mind of the Court by 'his old accusers', who had persuaded them in their childhood or youth that 'there was a person called Socrates, a wise man, a meditator on the things above us, and a researcher into all the secrets beneath the earth, who made the worse cause into the better. . . . And those who heard him and his companions thought that the men who made these researches did not believe in any God (οὐδὲ Θεοὺς νομίζειν). To fight against this false prejudice is like fighting a shadow (σκιαμαχεῖν); it will never come to grips.' A little later he says specifically: 'You yourselves have seen this in Aristophanes' comedy: a Socrates who is carried about and says that he walks the air and talks a great deal more nonsense of which I know nothing at all.'

How can we pretend, it may be asked, that the *Clouds* did not constitute a definite and fierce attack upon Socrates when Socrates himself thinks it largely caused his death? The danger, we should reply, came from the change in atmosphere. The charges quoted in the *Apology* as so damaging to Socrates are not grave charges. To sail aloft in a basket in order to observe the sun is not a crime; to study the things above us (τὰ μετέωρα) and to discover those beneath the earth is, in reasonable eyes, rather a credit than the reverse. One charge indeed remains; one that was added in the second version of the *Clouds* and which seems rather more serious. We must consider it more carefully.

To make the worse or weaker case appear the better or stronger is believed to be the special talent, or privilege, or crime, of a successful barrister. The belief explains why very good advocates obtain very high fees, and also why the plain man is from time to time swept by a flood of mistrust and aversion towards lawyers. There seems some reason to believe that some of the teachers of rhetoric did claim this dangerous power; but Socrates in the *Clouds* is never represented as a rhetorician, and the contest of the two *Logoi*, Just and Unjust, is not at all like a rivalry between two advocates in bamboozling a jury. It is a contest in Dialectic—διαλεκτική or ἀντιλογική, the regular Socratic method—between Morality and Immorality. The tone of it is exactly like the sophistic treatise called the *Dissoi Logoi*[1] or the Περὶ Ἀληθείας of Antiphon Sophista. The *Adikos Logos* admits at the opening that his is the worse case and deliberately proposes to make it win the argument. The charge, so far as there is a charge, against Socrates is not that he agrees with the *Adikos Logos*, or that the *Adikos Logos*, as such, is his pupil, but that his pupils are so trained in Dialectic that they can make black appear white if they try. There are plenty of passages in Plato which are open to this sort of charge, for every philosopher sometimes enjoys a paradox. And, though, taken in connexion with the burning of the Phrontisterion, it does suggest that, in his revision, Aristophanes was anxious to show that he was against the new learning and not for it, it does not in itself constitute a very serious attack on the character or honour of a philosopher.

The whole trouble and danger came from the change of atmosphere. In 423 these charges were jokes. In 399 they were not jokes at all. The Demos had just fought its way back to a city

---

[1] Found in the MSS. of Sextus Empiricus, and edited in Diels, *Vorsokratiker*, ii, p. 635.

which had been betrayed and subjected to a reign
of terror by men with whom Socrates had lived in
peace and intimacy, men who openly despised the
City's form of worship and were commonly held
to be atheists; men who were pupils of sophists, and
some of them pupils of Socrates himself; men whose
mysterious act of sacrilege towards the Hermae
was believed to have wrecked the Sicilian Expedition. One cannot wonder that a formidable wave
of hatred and fear welled up at this time against
all who were in any way 'wiser' than their fathers
or who dared to make researches into unknown
subjects. To make the worse appear the better
cause could be represented as a diabolical proceeding and the cause of all the disasters of the People
—the unhappy People, who had of course no
intellectual armour against the 'wisdom' of these
dreadful philosophers. Parallels will easily suggest
themselves. To have found a 'spiritual home' in
Germany was an innocent philosophical preference
in 1911; in 1915 it was a criminal perversity,
enough to drive Lord Haldane out of public life.
To believe in the perfectibility of mankind in 1780
was an amiable fad; fifteen years later it was held
to imply sympathy with the worst excesses of the
French Revolution and to justify loyal citizens in
burning Dr. Priestley's house down. There is certainly a great difference in the tone adopted towards the new learning, or the sophistic movement,
between, roughly speaking, 440 and 400 B.C. In

Aeschylus, in Herodotus, in the early plays of Euripides, in the *Antigone* (332 ff.), in the retrospective parts of Thucydides, in all that we know about Pericles and his circle, we find a spirit of confidence in the power of man by thought and skill and fearless speculation to create a better life for the individual and the city. Even in the early dialogues of Plato there is still a spirit of gay enjoyment in confounding the bourgeois and turning received ideas upside down. But the War was at work with its disasters, its brutality and cynicism, its revivals of superstition. We have the record of Thucydides' Melian Dialogue, of the cynical statesmen in Euripides' latest plays and some of the lyrics of the *Bacchae*; the outbursts against the wicked sophists in Plato's *Gorgias* and *Republic*; the arrangements for a religious inquisition and the execution of atheists in the *Laws*. A phrase that was a harmless jest in 423 might easily become deadly denunciation in 399. As Plato explains in the *Apology*, the old comedies had created a myth: Socrates was a sophist, he taught new doctrines, he did not worship the City's traditional gods but something else —undefined and therefore sinister; he pursued a practice of dialectic, of arguing about all questions, even the most fundamental, and putting the two sides of every case against each other. The good democratic citizens who had fought their way back to the City against the Tyrants knew what disasters that sort of man had brought upon Athens. They were not likely to let themselves be beguiled again by the same sophistries. None the less, such men were safer out of the way.

One cannot help wondering what Aristophanes was doing at the time of Socrates' trial in 399. Did he come forward as a witness to character, explaining how innocent had been the meaning of those twenty-four-year-old mockeries? Was he himself regarded by the extreme democrats as a suspicious character, whose support would do more harm than good? Or, again, since he was still of military age, was he away on garrison duty some-where, and not in Athens at all? It is in cases like this that one feels the terrible incompleteness of the evidence from which we have to construct our understanding of ancient history. We only know that, whatever he did, he did not lose Plato's friendship.

The two plays that were preferred to the *Clouds* were the *Pytînê*, or *Bottle*, of Cratînus and the *Connos* of Ameipsias. In the former the old wine-bibber represented himself as being threatened with divorce by his true wife, Comedy, because of his infidelities with Methê (Drink), and promising amends. (See above, p. 18.) The latter, however, had for its hero Connus, the music-master who taught Socrates, it introduced Socrates himself, and had a Chorus of Φροντισταί or Thinkers. Was this similarity of subject due to a mere coincidence, or to a previous agreement, or again are we to suppose that for some reason Socrates had particularly attracted public notice at that time and was, so to speak, the obvious subject for the current comic cartoon? The last seems the most probable explanation. If we look through the eight plays of Aristophanes which are furnished with full extracts from the Didascaliae, or, as we should say, full notices of the first performance, we find two similar cases. The *Frogs*, which presents a contest in poetry between Aeschylus and Euripides, had as one of its competitors the *Muses* of Phrynichus, which is believed on fairly good evidence to have shown the same sort of contest between Sophocles and Euripides, with a Chorus of the Muses as judges. In the *Birds* we have two Athenians so disgusted with the worries and troubles of life in Athens that they go to live among the birds in a cloud-city. One of the competing plays was the *Monotropos* or *Solitary* of Phrynichus, whose hero, from a similar disgust, leaves Athens and the haunts of mankind to live as a hermit. In the *Clouds*, too, we hear that when once Hyperbolus 'gave a handle' (παρεδώκεν λαβήν) in the year 421, and was made the hero of Eupolis' *Maricâs*, all the comedians fell upon him at once.

Thus the *Clouds* is not at all a passionate attack on some object which roused the poet's indignation, like the oppression of the Allies in the *Babylonians*, the war in the *Acharnians*, or the man

Cleon in the *Knights*. It is not quite like the *Wasps*, a strong attack on a monstrous system in which very decent people, whom Aristophanes liked, were involved. It is a study of a new and strange phenomenon which attracted and amused the clever poet: the teaching of this queer man, Socrates, with his intimate band of ascetic and utterly unworldly disciples and his outer circle of rich and fashionable and probably unprincipled καλοκάγαθοί. Aristophanes has studied Socrates with almost the same care and interest that he afterwards devoted to Euripides, and has invented a good foil for him. The foil has to be ignorant and stupid because Socrates is learned and acute; country-bred because Socrates is of the city; and lastly a rogue or 'twister', with his mind concentrated on dollars, because Socrates had no thought at all of such things. The poet realized that his play was not a play for the multitude; it had mainly an intellectual appeal; but he trusted in the intellectual quality of his judges, and was sharply disappointed when the piece failed. He rewrote it and in particular added two scenes which are much more hostile to Socrates and definitely condemn him and his teaching. I can best explain this by supposing that, for some reason, he attributed the failure of the play to its having left the impression of being favourable to Socrates and his 'new education': consequently he was determined to correct that impression and insist that

he stood squarely where he had stood in the
Daitalês, for the Old Training and against the
New. Probably the changes rather damaged the
play than improved it. It is not perhaps a very
good play. Compared with the *Acharnians* or the
Wasps it is not really very funny, nor compared
with the *Knights* very exciting. Yet it remains
a social document of extraordinary interest. It
gives us a contemporary character-sketch of one
of the most remarkable men in human history and
a vivid picture of the eternal strife between Old
and New as waged more than two thousand years
ago among the ideas of an age as troubled as our
own.

CHAPTER V

LITERATURE: EURIPIDES
(Acharnians, 425; *Thesmophoriazusae,* 410 (?);
Frogs, 405)

ARISTOPHANES was after all first and foremost a
man of letters. As a writer of comedy he was
σοφός and could not altogether get on with the
spectators who were not σοφοί also. His first quarrel
with the new education was its neglect of literature. Even his politics are the politics of a literary
man, greatly moved by the spirit of a policy, its
cruelty, its unfairness, its vulgarity, and not so
much by its material results. His wildest scenes
of farce never get far away from literature; they
abound in parodies and quotations and are often
actually founded on some scene in a tragedy. He
quotes, at a rough calculation, no less than twenty-
one writers, mostly poets, of previous generations,
from Homer to Aeschylus, and mentions about
double that number of contemporaries. He loved all
poetry; he loved perverting it and laughing at it. But
above all poetry he knew by heart and quoted and
parodied and mocked at the tragedies of Euripides.

One must always remember that Comedy originated in a traditional half-magic ritual, one of
those rites, common to most primitive societies,
which are themselves part of the sacred laws and
customs by which our fathers lived, and which

make it their aim and their excuse to preserve those laws and customs. To honour and obey the City's Gods, the City's laws, and one's own parents, was, according to Greek traditional ideas, the whole duty of man. To do so was Themis: to fail to do so was a breach of Themis, and might have quite unpredictable consequences. Hence Aristophanes, and, as far as we can judge, the other comedians, are normally defenders of the established custom, and satirize all that is new or unusual. Hence also the chief character in Aristophanes is almost always an Old Man, a γέρων, who knows and likes the old ways, whereas young men, poor creatures, usually do not know what is Themis and what not! It is only natural, therefore, that Comedy finds its obvious prey in new teachers, like Socrates, in innovating poets, like Euripides, in startling ideas, like this fancy of the philosophers about the equality of women and men.

It is difficult for us, and would have been difficult for Aristophanes himself, to say exactly what his feelings were towards Euripides and his poetry. He certainly was fascinated by it. It haunted his memory and imagination, and he parodied it with a charm and skill which prove his enjoyment and understanding. At the same time he almost certainly disapproved of it, or at least felt officially bound to disapprove of it, just as he disapproved of Socrates, and the sophistic movement in general, and all this nonsense about women . . . though, to be sure, if women had their way, Greece might still be saved! So he writes the *Clouds*, and the *Lysistrata*, and diligently studies Euripides till a rival comedian, Cratînus, mocks at him for writing in the same refined, epigrammatic over-intellectual style, and coins the word 'Euripidaristophanism'.[1]

Considering the extreme generosity with which Aristophanes distributes personal abuse when so disposed, it is interesting to note that there is no attack on the personal character or honour of Euripides. We observed the same with regard to Socrates. One of the less pleasing accusations which are freely tossed about in the Old Comedy, for example, is that of personal immorality. It is probably part of the phallic ritual, and means little. It is flung most emphatically at Agathon, for example, when he is found rehearsing his verses at the opening of the *Thesmophoriazusae*, but the insult did not prevent Aristophanes from being one of the chosen guests at Agathon's famous Symposium, nor from passing the kindly judgement upon him in the *Frogs*: 'A true poet, whom his many friends miss deeply'. So it is the more striking that no personal attack of that sort, or indeed of any other sort, is made against Euripides: no charge of immorality, of softness, of taking bribes, of avarice, of cowardice, of 'sycophancy', or anything else. The most that one can say is that

---

[1] Cratinus, fr. 307: τίς δὲ σὺ κομψός (πᾶς ἄν τις ἔροιτο θεατής), | ὑπολεπτο-λόγος, γνωμοδιώκτης, Εὐριπιδαριστοφανίζων;

in the contest with Aeschylus in the *Frogs* Euripides is made rather conceited and unpleasant.

We possess three plays in which Euripides comes in for special attention. In 425 B.C., at the opening of his career as a comedian, Aristophanes devotes one whole scene of the *Acharnians* to him. Fifteen years later, in the *Thesmophoriazusae*, he creates scene after scene of ingenious farce almost entirely out of lines from three Euripidean tragedies. Lastly, in 405, after the poet's death, Aristophanes represents the God of Drama, Dionysus, as descending to Hades to fetch Euripides back, since he is unable to live without him, but eventually deciding that, if one and one only of the great poets of the past is to come back, he would sooner have Aeschylus. This play gives Aristophanes occasion to make a long study of Euripides' work as a dramatic poet, and to enrich us with the liveliest and most intimate piece of literary criticism that has come down from antiquity.

In the *Acharnians* Dicaiopolis, the 'Honest Citizen', has obtained permission to make one speech in defence of himself and his pacifism before he is stoned to death by the patriotic charcoal-burners of Acharnae, and he naturally wishes to move their pity. The great man for moving pity is Euripides. Dicaiopolis will go to him and ask for the costume and properties of one of his ruined and outcast kings, who always plunge the theatre into tears. 'Is Euripides at home?' 'At home and not at home', says his servant, who partakes of his master's refined intellectualism; 'his mind is abroad gathering verses, but his body is upstairs.' Can he come down? He has no leisure to come down, but eventually consents to be 'rolled out' on a Machine, like a God in one of his own tragedies. He is dressed pitifully, in rags, since he is writing about one of his broken and outcast heroes. It is just rags that Dicaiopolis wants, some particular very ragged rags, very moving, but he cannot remember the hero's name. 'Was it Oineus, that aged man of sorrows?' No; much worse. 'The blind Phoinix, perhaps?' Worse than Phoinix. 'The beggar Philoctêtês, then?' Oh, a much more beggarish beggar than Philoctêtês. 'The crippled Bellerophon?' No; though my man was lame, too, and very very talkative. 'Oh, of course, Têlephus!' And Têlephus it was. His rags are found lying between those of Thyestes and Ino, and are duly lent to the petitioner. Still, however, Dicaiopolis needs a few further 'properties' to complete the outfit of a perfect Euripidean outcast: a cap, a staff, a lamp-basket, a cup with a broken lip, an earthenware bottle corked with a sponge, some dried leaves and finally

> Inferior cabbage, fresh from Mother's arms!
> (σκάνδικά μοι δός, μητρόθεν δεδεγμένος.)

to which the answer is, in true tragic style:

> The man presumeth. Bar the castle doors!
> (ἀνὴρ ὑβρίζει· κλῇε πηκτὰ δωμάτων.)[1]

---

[1] It was for some reason a joke to pretend that Euripides' mother,

As comedy the scene is admirable, but as criticism it is not very clear. Did Euripides give himself airs? Did he dress in tragic dress like his own heroes when he was composing tragedy, as Agathon in the *Thesmophoriazûsae* dressed like his heroine (*Thesm.* 148 ff.), or as, according to Dumas, Wagner dressed in medieval costume when composing a medieval opera? It seems improbable. Did he really dress his beggared and outcast kings in rags and give them the staff and scrip of beggars? We know that no tragic poet did so, though it is likely enough that when necessary for the plot, he did introduce some modification in the extreme stateliness of the tragic dress, as Sophocles also did in the *Philoctêtês*. In all probability his costumes would have seemed to us terribly conventional and unnatural; to his contemporaries, accustomed to something stiffer still, they apparently gave the impression of daring realism. The main impression that emerges from the scene is of an incongruity somewhere. Is it between the alleged grubby realism of the dress and properties on the one hand and the lofty tragic diction on the other? 'Take it, and get thee from my marble halls', does seem wrong when 'it' is a sort of tramp's walking-stick; yet in other passages it is

Cleito, was a greengrocer, and that her greens were 'wild', not the proper garden variety.

Wild are the wrongs he does us:
Was he not reared among wild cabbages? (*Thesm.* 455–6.)

σκάνλιξ, 'chervil', was an ἄγριον λάχανον.

the homely diction of Euripides that is particularly criticized. The real clash is not between dress and diction, but between the whole effort of Euripides to get closer to real life and this stiff tragic convention, with its priestly dress and its magic masks, in which he was bound to work. That, I should say, is a true criticism. There is no doubt an incongruity in Euripides' art somewhere, as there must almost always be in the work of a pioneer.

In the *Thesmophoriazûsae,* or *Women Keeping the Thesmophoria,* which was not produced till the year 411 or 410, Euripides is actually one of the principal characters. He enters with his 'relative by marriage',[1] Mnesilochus, who is the *scurra senex,* or 'Elderly Jester' of the piece. In highly philosophical language Euripides explains the situation to Mnesilochus. The women of Athens, indignant at the constant revelations of their secret thoughts and misdoings by Euripides, are about to take advantage of their private festival, the Thesmophoria, from which men are excluded, to plan his death. He has come to beseech his fellow artist Agathon, who is smooth-faced, soft, and fair, to go disguised among the women and discover their plans. Agathon, who is rolled out upon a Machine, as Euripides was in the *Acharnians,* and is actually dressed at the moment like one of his heroines— ('I used to be like that once!' says Euripides)—

---

[1] κηλέστης (not γαμβρός or πενθερός). Mnesilochus seems to have been a recurrent name in the family of Euripides' wife, Melito.

refuses in language that is none the less firm for being philosophical. Euripides is in despair, when old Mnesilochus in a comic gush of generous affection undertakes to go himself. The disguise is less satisfactory in his case. But they borrow from Agathon a female costume and a razor, and painfully shave the hairy old man. Euripides swears—'with his heart and not his tongue'[1]—not to desert him, and Mnesilochus goes in to the feast. The scene changes to the temple of the Thesmophorô—the two goddesses presiding over the day. There are various rites and prayers. Mnesilochus mingles successfully with the crowd. At last the subject of Euripides is introduced, and a woman, Micca, makes a speech against him. 'He analyses our feelings, he puts the most dreadful ideas into our menfolk's heads. If·a woman breaks a cup, if she has a headache, if she looks pale, she must have a secret lover. By these suspicions he has taken away all our freedom. He must die.' She is seconded by a garland-seller, whose trade has collapsed—like that of Demetrius the silversmith in Ephesus—since Euripides has persuaded people not to believe in the gods. The disguised Mnesilochus now rises for the defence. 'Of course Euripides has said many bad things of women, quite true. But just think of the things he might have said and did not! How I sent my husband

---

[1] A reference to the much-quoted line in the *Hippolytus*, '"Twas but my tongue, 'twas not my heart that swore!'

to the kitchen to make a warming medicine for me, because I felt ill, while I went out to meet my old lover in the garden. How a friend of mine smuggled her lover out of the house behind a shawl which she held up for her husband to admire. Then think of all the tricks by which we buy babies to pass off as our own!' The speech is causing lively trouble when Cleisthenes—the beardless friend of women—comes in with the news that the sanctity of the festival has been violated: a man is said to have got in in disguise. There is a search, and in spite of his protests ('What! Would you undress a mother of nine?'), Mnesilochus is discovered. He is made prisoner and the women send for the police. Meantime a woman keeps guard.

During the parabasis the prisoner thinks of Euripides and his resourceful heroes. When Palamêdês, for instance, was a prisoner before Troy he sent word to his father by writing on oar-blades which he threw into the sea. Mnesilochus has not any oar-blades handy, but writes on the votive tablets that are hanging up in the temple, and throws them abroad, to the accompaniment of lyrics from the *Palamêdês*. Apparently one of them reaches its destination, for we find that Euripides knows that his agent is a prisoner, though he does not yet make his appearance. Disappointed with the *Palamêdês*, Mnesilochus begins to quote the *Helena*:

These are the fair-nymphed waters of the Nile. . . .
And I was Helen!

('At it again?', says the woman guarding him. 'I
should have thought you had had enough of pretending to be a woman.')

Now I linger here,

But Menelaus, my unhappy lord,

Still comes not!

Enter EURIPIDES *as Menelaus.*

EUR. Who is the tyrant of these frowning walls?

And what strange land is this?

MNE. This is the palace of King Proteus, Sir,

In Egypt.

('Don't believe a word he says', exclaims the guard.)

EUR. And wherefore sit'st thou on this monument,

Veiled in thy mantle, princess?

MNE. They compel me,

A weeping bride, to wed with Proteus' son.

('Good gentleman', says the guard, 'it's all quite
untrue. He is a bad man who came here in disguise
to steal things.')

In spite of the guard's warnings the scene proceeds to a passionate and astonished Recognition
between Menelaus and Helen; Menelaus attempts
to carry home his long-lost wife, but the guard,
though bewildered, will not stand this, and Euripides retires defeated. A Superintendent of Police
now enters and puts the prisoner in charge of a
much tougher guardian, a Scythian archer, such
as formed the ordinary police force of Athens.
Mnesilochus is tied to a plank—the equivalent of
the stocks—and so exposed in his woman's dress.
He is falling into despair when he sees a figure
flying—by means of a tragic Mêchanê—through

the air. It is Euripides disguised as Perseus. Taking the hint, Mnesilochus immediately becomes Andromeda, chained to the rock, and starts on the opening scene of the play so named, in which the heroine, alone amid the sea rocks, has a lyrical scene with Echo. Echo repeats the last words of Andromeda, and also, with great effect, the last broken Greek of the Scythian, till the barbarian is completely bewildered. Enter Euripides as Perseus. Perseus sees the chained princess,

> A vision beautiful as shapes divine!
> O Maid, I pity thee.

'It isn't a girl, it's a sinful old man', (οὐ παρτέν' ἐστίν, ἀλλ' ἀμαρτωλὴ γέρων) gibbers the Scythian, but in vain. Perseus, gazing on the prisoner, is seized with love for her at first sight—much to the Scythian's surprise—and is proceeding at once to cut her bonds, when the Scythian draws his sword and puts a stop to that.

Escape seems impossible, but Euripides now enters and proposes terms to the Chorus of Women. He will never speak ill of them again if they will let him save his relative from the Scythian. They agree, and he returns presently disguised as an old woman, Artemisia, with a young dancing girl, who has to practise for a public performance. The girl's shoe comes undone, she must sit down to fasten it up, and there is nothing to sit upon but the Scythian's knee. The Scythian kindly helps with the shoe, is fascinated, and eventually goes

off the stage for a moment with the girl, leaving
the old woman to watch the prisoner. In a moment
the bonds are cut and Euripides and Mnesilochus
run off. The Scythian comes back, is horrified
at the wicked conduct of the old woman, and runs
off in the wrong direction shouting for 'Arte-
mouxia' in unintelligible Greek.

Is there any attack or any criticism here? On
the whole it is difficult to see how Euripides can
have regarded the *Thesmophoriazûsae* as anything
but a tremendous compliment. It shows immense
interest in his writings; it implies that they were
known by every one, and that parodies of them, or
even allusions to them, would be instantly recognized and make people laugh. It is worth noticing,
also, not only that the verses themselves are often
charming, but that while most of the other characters in the play are exhibited in grotesque and
humiliating positions, Euripides is spared. Agathon
is treated with scant respect; the various women are
tipplers or worse; the Scythian is a laughing-stock;
Mnesilochus goes through every stage of ridiculous
humiliation; but Euripides has on the whole the
beau rôle. He is faithful to his friend, he invents one
plan after another, and ultimately he triumphs. Of
course he is chaffed for an over-philosophic manner, and one is not sure that 'the most tragic of the
poets' would feel unmixed pride at the compliment:

τοῦ γὰρ τεχνάζειν ἡμέτερος ὁ πυραμοῦς.
As far as dodges go, we take the cake!

But in the main the play is rather a tribute to the great fame of Euripides than an attack on him.

What was, then, at the end of the count, Aristophanes' real opinion about Euripides? He had quoted him, advertised him, laughed at him and with him for so many years, and at last the great poet was dead and his place empty. In 405 Aristophanes tried to sum up what he had to say about Euripides. It is a surprise to us, when we think of it, to realize that an Athenian audience could sit through long scenes of literary criticism and parody devoted to the comparison of two dead tragedians, and at the end not merely pronounce the play worthy of the first prize, but actually insist on a repetition of the performance a few days later. The *Frogs* was probably the greatest success Aristophanes ever achieved, yet he clearly knew the risk he was running. The *Clouds* had been above the heads of the audience; will not this be more so? 'No', he makes the Chorus say: 'if you fear that the audience may be a little stupid, and miss the points of your subtleties, do not be anxious: that is no longer likely. They have been through the training. Every one of them has his book, and understands what is good taste.' The whole intellectual level of the audience had risen; Aristophanes, the intellectual farce-writer, has profited by it; and the cause of the whole improvement has been that 'new learning' of which Euripides is the champion.

What is the main plot of the *Frogs*? When the *Frogs* was writing, it would appear, Sophocles was still alive, though he died before the actual performance. But Euripides was dead, and the world seemed empty and tasteless without him— at least that was the feeling of Dionysus, the divine patron of drama. He must have a poet—a real poet with power to create (γόνιμον ποιητήν) and will to dare. He goes to Hades to bring back Euripides, and, after many adventures, arrives there to find a contest going on between Euripides and the ancient Aeschylus, who has held the Throne of Poetry ever since his death. The contest proceeds, with Dionysus as judge. There is mutual criticism of the general style of both poets; then of prologues; then of lyrics of various kinds; then of the weight of individual verses. Still, Dionysus will not decide. He loves both men. He wants to be friends with both. One is so accomplished (σοφός), and he does so enjoy the other. At last, in the hope of getting more light, he asks the two their advice about the public affairs of Athens; the question is not entirely irrelevant, since both rivals have accepted the view that a poet is to be judged by his wisdom and the advice he gives (1009). The pressing problem of the moment is Alcibiades. What do the two poets say about him? Euripides condemns the man who 'is slow to help and quick

to injure his country, rich in resources for himself
and bankrupt for her'. Aeschylus differs: 'It is
wiser not to rear a lion's whelp; but if you have
reared one, you must accept its ways.' The judge
is still doubtful. What advice have they for the
City; how can she be saved? 'Put your trust where
mistrust is,' says Euripides, 'and mistrust where
you now put trust.' That is, turn out the present
advisers and call back the wiser, more cultivated
and more moderate leaders—whom Aristophanes
also believed in. And what says Aeschylus? 'Treat
the enemy's land as yours, and yours as the
enemy's; your ships as your treasure and. your
"new treasure" as despair.' The words are an
expression of the old policy of Pericles (Thuc.
i. 143) suited for more prosperous times than 405.
At any rate they clearly imply war *jusqu'au bout*.
Live on your enemy's land, think no more about
your own, put all your hopes in your fleet, and—
apparently, though not certainly—recognize that
you are financially ruined and that the new special
taxes will bring no help.[1]

'Come, give your decision,' says Pluto. And
Dionysus, with a plunge, giving up the attempt
at a critical judgement, says he will choose the one
he happens to like; Aeschylus! One can hardly

---

[1] The passage 1437–66 seems to contain a mixture of alternative
versions. I have provisionally accepted the view of the ancient critics,
Aristarchus and Apollodorus; but there is much to be said for Van
Leeuwen's suggestion that 1460–6 come from a speech of Pericles in
Eupolis' *Demoi*.

imagine a closer contest; and when one realizes
that the contest is for the supreme throne of poetry
it is difficult to suppose that the *Frogs* was written
as a mere attack on Euripides or an attempt to
show that he was a bad poet. William James
speaks somewhere of a man who threatened suicide
because he was only the second-best baseball
'striker' in the world; only by such a standard as
that can the *Frogs* be regarded as a condemnation
of Euripides. It is something far more natural and
far more interesting. Euripides was dead; the
world seemed empty of poetry. Oh, if one could
go down to the grave and bring him back! And
yet, if one could do that; if one could bring back
from Hades one poet and only one, would it be
Euripides, or are there greater poets still? Is there
not he whom we loved and worshipped in childhood, old-fashioned perhaps and despised by the
critics of to-day, not quite to be defended on
sophisticated modern standards, but still incom-
parable, the King of poets, Aeschylus!

So much for the general scheme of the play; but
there are also a great number of minute and
definite criticisms which have to be considered.
Some are mere jokes; for of course we must
remember that we are dealing not merely with a
comedy, but a comedy in the ancient sense—a wild
though highly intellectual farce—and cannot take
all its quips seriously. For example, it is said that
the burglars and thieves were all on the side of

Euripides because of τῶν ἀντιλογιῶν καὶ λυγισμῶν καὶ στροφῶν (771), where στροφαί mean both 'twists' and 'strophes', λυγισμοί both 'changing tones of voice' and 'wrestling tricks', and the ἀντιλογίαι or 'controversies' in which Euripides excelled are very different from the 'denials' with which the said criminals liked to meet accusations. Similarly when Aeschylus refuses to compete on the ground that his poetry has not died with him, so that he has none by him, while that of Euripides is all dead and handy, it is a joke and no more (869).

Another quite absurd joke has been taken seriously by commentators. Euripides is quoting his prologues, and Aeschylus threatens to destroy the whole lot of them with a ληκύθιον, or 'oil-flask', of the sort that was commonly carried and served both for anointing the body and for mixing paints.[1] Euripides quotes seven prologues, and in

---

[1] In my first version I made the oil-flask into an old umbrella.

A. By Zeus, I won't go pecking word by word
    At every phrase. I'll take one old umbrella,
    God helping me, and smash your prologues whole.

E. My prologues . . . with umbrellas?

A.   One umbrella.
    You write them so that nothing comes amiss,
    The bed-quilt or the umbrella, or the clothes-bag,
    All suit your tragic verse. Wait and I'll prove it.

    . . . . . .

E. 'Aegyptus, so the world-wide tale is spread,
    When o'er the waves with fifty sons he fled
    To Argos,'   (From *Archelaus*.)

A.   found his old umbrella gone.

    . . . . . .

[*Footnote continued on opposite page.*

six of them, before he has finished the third line,
Aeschylus interjects the words ληκύθιον ἀπώλεσε,
'lost his little flask of oil', so as to complete both
sense and metre.

The effect is very funny, but the criticism
amounts to nothing. Scholars say that it indicates
the monotony of Euripides' versification, but this
is simply not the case. As a matter of fact, of the
seven prologues quoted the seventh—the funniest
—does not really work; the sixth, according to the
Scholiast, was not taken from the beginning of the
Meleager, but from a passage some way on; the
first did not agree with the version of the *Archelaus*
which the Scholiast knew. And further, among the
tragedies that have come down to us the ληκύθιον
tag does not fit the openings of Euripides any more

E. 'Dionysus, who with wand and fawnskin dight,
   On great Parnassus dances in the light
   Of torches,'   (*Hypsipyle.*)
A.   found his old umbrella gone.

   A little later we have:
E. 'King Oineus' . . .
A.   found his old umbrella gone.
E. You must first let me quote one line entire!
   'King Oineus, for a goodly harvest won,
   While praying' . . .   (*Meleager.*)
                 found his old umbrella gone.
D. (During the prayers? Who can have been the thief?)

   At last we have:
E. Enough! I challenge him to answer this!
   'Great Zeus in heaven, the word of truth is flown . . .'
                                   (*Melanippe the Wise.*)
D. Oh, stop him!—His is certain to be gone.

than those of Sophocles or Aeschylus.[1] There is, as criticism, simply nothing in it; yet, such was the influence of this scene that the particular metre of ληκύθιον ἀπώλεσε, i.e. the second part of an iambic

[1] EURIPIDES.

Heracl. Πάλαι ποτ' ἐστὶ τοῦτ' ἐμοὶ Δελογμένον·
ὁ μὲν Δίκαιος . . . ληκύθιον ἀπώλεσε.

Hec. Ἥκω, νεκρῶν κευθμῶνα καὶ σκότου πύλας
λιπών, ἵν' Ἅιδης . . . ληκύθιον ἀπώλεσε.

Phoen. 7 would work, but the seventh line is too far on to count.

SOPHOCLES.

Aj. 4. Αἴαντος, ἔνθα . . . ληκύθιον ἀπώλεσε.

O.T. 4. Πόλις Δ' ὁμοῦ μὲν . . . ληκύθιον ἀπώλεσε.

Better is the *Antigone*:

Ὦ κοινὸν αὐτάδελφον Ἰσμήνης κάρα,
ἆρ' οἶσθ' ὅτι Ζεὺς . . . ληκύθιον ἀπώλεσε;

and *Trach.* 3. Λόγος μὲν ἔστ' ἀρχαῖος ἀνθρώπων φανείς,
ὡς οὐκ ἂν αἰῶν' ἐκμάθοις βροτῶν, πρὶν ἂν
θάνη τις, οὔτ' εἰ . . . ληκύθιον ἀπώλεσε.

AESCHYLUS.

The opening of the *Eumenides* is good:

Πρῶτον μὲν εὐχῇ τῇδε πρεσβεύω θεῶν
τὴν πρωτόμαντιν Γαῖαν· ἐκ Δὲ τῆς Θέμιν,
ἣ Δὴ τὸ μητρὸς . . . ληκύθιον ἀπώλεσε.

Mr. J. D. Denniston, however, writes: 'I believe there is a serious criticism underlying the foolery of the ληκύθιον episode. If you set yourself the task, as Euripides did, of telling the back-history of a play succinctly in the opening scene, you will, in a periodic language like Greek, almost certainly start somehow like this: "John Jones, of Bradford, having emigrated to Florida and made a fortune in orange-growing, finding, on his return home, that his wife had absconded with another man, consults his solicitor." I think the rules of the game are that you start with a proper name, and then, after a line or two of subordinate clauses, round off metre and sense with a ληκύθιον. As a matter of fact, Euripides nearly always starts as far from mere narrative as he possibly can, with an apostrophe, a gnome or the like. The ληκύθιον represents not what he often does in fact, but what he would do every time if he were not careful!'

trimeter after the ordinary caesura (—∪—∪—∪—,
'found his old umbrella gone') was subsequently
called not only ληκύθιον, which was more or less
justified, but Εὐριπίδειον, which was absurd.

As for the serious criticisms, they are hard to
seize, but in the main they resolve themselves into
breaches of Themis and the consequent incongruities. The two spheres in which all primitive
societies are specially subject to taboos are religion
and sex, and Euripides, like Socrates, was not satis-
fied with the Greek conventions about either. Then
tragedy itself was in origin a religious rite which
ought according to Themis to be composed in a
certain way, whereas Euripides was always making
experiments with it. True, he was very intellectual
and full of conscious artistic principles; but... well,
Aristophanes really preferred Aeschylus, who
simply wrote as he ought, without knowing why.

The idea of scientific literary criticism was new
and 'Euripidean'. He would weigh the poetry
line by line; measure it with straight edges, mitre-
squares, cubit-rules and frames... a method which
made Aeschylus 'stoop and glower like a mad bull'.
He would produce work that was ἀστεῖον, urba-
num, κατερρινημένον, lima perpolitum; above all, lucid
(900 ff., 945 ff., 1122); whereas Aeschylus wrote
for an audience fresh from Phrynichus and only
half-civilized. His diction, though far more varied
than that of Aeschylus, tries to be appropriate: he
would not use the word ἀλεκτρυών, cock, in a

tragedy, as Aeschylus did.[1] And he is fluent,
terribly fluent: he can express himself on any
subject (στωμύλος, λάλος, 91, 841; *Ach.* 429, &c.).
In manner too, he is conceited and 'superior', as
the intellectual mostly seems to the low-brow. He
can not only speak himself, but he makes all his
characters do so.

E. Next, I taught all the town to talk with freedom.
A.   I admit it.
   'Twere better, ere you taught them you had died amid
      their curses!
E. I gave them canons to apply and squares for marking
      verses;
   Taught them to see, think, understand, to scheme for
      what they wanted,
   To fall in love, think evil, question all things. . . .
A.   Granted, granted!

This is still the intellectual criticized by the plain
man. The intellectual applies canons of criticism;
he also has a much wider range of thought and
discussion than the plain man thinks safe or proper
or even intelligible. He does teach his disciples to
'see, think, understand' and perhaps also to 'question all things'—certainly Socrates did: and is easily
accused of teaching them to scheme, to give too
much thought to love, and to 'think evil'. This
charge is made definite later on. Euripides has
not only produced his Phaedras and Stheneboeas,

[1] Aeschylus, it is worth noting, carefully avoids using the word in
Eumenides, 866 ἐνοικίου δ' ὄρνιθος οὐ λέγω μάχην.

he has actually dared to introduce go-betweens
on the tragic stage!

What hasn't he done that is under the sun,
And the love-dealing dames that with him have begun?
   One's her own brother's wife,
   One says 'Life is not Life',
And one goes into shrines to give birth to a son!
(1078 ff.)

The 'go-between' was perhaps the Nurse in the
Hippolytus; in the *Aeolus*, Macareus was in love
with his sister Canacê; Augê the priestess, ravished
by Heracles, bore her child in the temple, praying
Athena's aid, and was cursed for her sacrilege. It
is part of the joke that Aeschylus classes with these
offences a thought which recurs in two beautiful
passages of Euripides, that perhaps this life on
earth is not our true life.

   Who knoweth if the thing that we call Death
   Be life, and our life dying? Who knoweth?

Such sentiments may not be actually wicked, but
they are all new-fangled and tiresome and wrong!
They are the sort of thing that has actually made
women commit suicide (1051)! Aeschylus claims
that Euripides in this way has corrupted his
generation:

Just think what they were when he had them from me!
   Good six-footers, solid of limb,
Well-born, well-bred, not ready to fly from obeying
   their country's call,

Nor in latter-day fashion to loiter and lie, and keep their
consciences small.
Their life was in shafts of ash and of elm, in bright
plumes fluttering wide,
In lance and greaves and corslet and helm, and hearts
of seven-fold hide.

On which Dionysus—or according to some editors,
Euripides—remarks:

Oh, now he's begun, and will probably run a whole
armourer's shop on my head!

Was it really the solid six-footer, with no thought
beyond his armour and the next battle, that made
the greatest and best kind of Athenian? And did
Aristophanes really think it was? A little later
Aeschylus complains that Euripides and his like
have taught

the crews of the pick of the ships
To answer back pat to their officer's nose; how unlike
my old sailor of yore,
With no thought in his head but to guzzle his brose, and
sing as he bent at the oar!

Even that description scarcely suggests the highest
type of Athenian sailor; but Dionysus adds other
characteristics:

And drop dirt on the head of the rowers below, and
garrotte stray lubbers ashore,
While our new man just sails where it happens to blow,
and argues, and rows no more.

So evidently the old sailor was not in Aristophanes'

eyes altogether an ideal type. (Cf. 965 ff., 1039, on the respective pupils of the two poets.)

There is another criticism which is hard to estimate. The complaint sometimes takes the form that Euripides is too *terre à terre* and realistic. He himself claims that he has 'put things on the stage that came from daily life and business, where the audience could catch him if he tripped' (959ff.). His opponents, going further, say that his tragedies are full of beggar's staves, old hats, broken pots, and bottles without the cork, not to speak of 'the bed-quilt, or the oil-flask or the clothes-bag', and make him wail, when these are taken from him, 'Man, you have robbed me of my tragedy'. In the *Frogs* he claims, like Wordsworth, that he has simplified and clarified the language of tragedy, which came to him swollen and feverish from the hands of Aeschylus. Yet, at the same time, Aristophanes in scores of passages parodies not the simplicity or prose-like quality of his diction, but its high-flown tragic grandeur or its lyrical or romantic daring. The fact is that Euripides widened the whole range of tragedy. He made it more close to life and clearer in expression, but also more romantic, adventurous and varied both in incident and in diction; and lastly he was a very great lyric poet. The parodies show him now a realist, now a tragedian of the pompous style, and now a peculiarly melodious and dreamy singer. The very musicalness of his verse is made a charge against

him. The ancients, who were perhaps more sensitive than we to the psychological effects of music,
seem constantly to associate subtlety and melodious-
ness of rhythm with sensuality. Agathon's lyrics
at the beginning of the *Thesmophoriazusae* are not
only like 'the walking of ants', but are greeted by
Mnesilochus with the exclamation:

What melting words! And, as I heard them sung,
Ye amorous powers, there crept upon my soul
A pleasant dreamy rapturous titillation. (Rogers.)

Yet there is not a word in them even remotely
approaching the amorous. So in the *Frogs* (1327)
a very musical and nonsensical parody of Euripides,
with some irregularities of metre but none of
morals, reminds Aeschylus of the notorious 'dozen
tricks' of the courtesan Cyrene, and seems to
demand the bones rather than the lyre for its
accompaniment.

> Ye halcyons, by the dancing sea
> Who babble everlastingly,
>   While on your bathing pinions fall
> The dewy foam-sprays, fresh and free;
>   And Oh, ye spiders, deft to crawl
>   In many a chink of roof and wall,
> While left and right, before, behind,
> Your fingers wi-i-i-i-ind
>   The treasures of the labouring loom,
> Fruit of the shuttle's minstrel mind,
> Where many a songful dolphin trips
> To lead the dark-blue-beakèd ships,

And tosses, with aërial touch,
Temples and race-courses and such.
O bright grape-tendril's essence pure,
Wine to sweep care from human lips!
Grant me, O Child, one arm-pressúre. . . .

At which point Aeschylus breaks off to denounce
the metrical licence of the last line. The verses
certainly 'babble'; that is, they run trippingly
and bewilderingly on into nonsense; the metre is
slightly, very slightly, irregular; more serious in
Aristophanes' eyes, the first syllable of εἱλίσσω,
'wind', instead of having one musical note to itself,
as in the strict old Greek music, is prolonged into
a whole series of notes—a roulade. This does not
suggest to our modern minds any grave under-
mining of morality. Nor does the parody of a
Euripidean monody, or solo, which follows. It is
too long to quote, but treats, with impassioned
language and much variety of style, of the escape
or theft of a cock from the singer's yard. She was
suspecting no evil, but quietly wi-i-i-i-inding her
wool, when

> He rose, rose in the air,
> On quivering blades of flight;
> He left me care, care,
> And tears, tears of despair,
> Fell, fell, and dimmed my sight.

However, by the help of Hecate, Dictynna, and
the Cretan Corybantes she hopes to recover him.

These are the best parodies in Aristophanes.

They are really like Euripides, and have a touch
of Euripidean loveliness in the midst of their
absurdity, whereas the parodies of Aeschylus,
which follow, are only strings of quotations incon-
gruously put together. At any rate they enable us
to see what Aristophanes criticized in the diction
and the metre, though unfortunately not in the
music. The incriminated music is lost to us, and
we find it hard to understand how intensely the
Greeks of this particular period felt about the
changes of musical style which were then taking
place.[1]

[1] Plato's strong feelings on the subject are well known, but a passage
in the *Cheiron* of Pherecrates (145), very obscure in detail but clear
enough in its general bearing, is the *locus classicus* in Comedy. *Music*,
an unfortunate woman with a varied past, is telling to *Justice* the story
of her wrongs, roughly thus:

MUSIC. I'll gladly tell you. It's a comfort, dear,
To tell you, and I know you'll like to hear.
The thing began with Melanippides:
He was my first. He caught me at his ease,
And left my strings all flabby. All the same
He wasn't bad, compared with some of them.
The next was that Athenian—whom God curse—
Kinêsias, with his twistings and his verse
All out of time with the music. He has quite
Destroyed me. In his dithyrambs the right
Looks like the left—like soldiers with cold feet!
Still, I could do with him, in spite of it.
Then Phrynis brought in his new whirligig
And twisted me and bent me like a twig—
Bah, him and his twelve moods on seven strings!
Still, even he. . . . If he did many things
All wrong, still he repaired them. But, my dear!
Timotheos! It's a corpse upon a bier

[*Footnote continued on opposite page.*

It looks as if the whole matter were mostly one of convention and association. One might have expected, if our critic was bent on denouncing the moral atmosphere of Euripides, that he would attack his *Ionic a minore* lyrics, which, so far as metre goes, are clearly more sensuous and passionate than these simple glyconics. But no; the Ionic metres had been used by Aeschylus and Phrynichus, and Aristophanes merely found them 'as sweet as honey' (*Wasps* 220). They were in the correct tragic tradition.

Only one of the tests to which the two poets are submitted brings out a clear result, the weighing of the verses. When all is said and done, the poetry of Aeschylus, verse by verse, weighs more and counts more. Euripides is eminently accomplished (σοφός). He has introduced numerous improvements into tragedy, he has removed many unskilfulnesses and flaws; he has made the range wider, the plots more ingenious, the characters more subtle and far more varied. He has made things articulate which in Aeschylus were confused and half-dumb. His Chorus, in place of the interminable discussions of theology with which

He has made me—scraped my life out! It's a shame!
JUSTICE. Timotheos?
MUSIC.   Of Miletus. That's his name;
A red-haired man. He is worse than all the rest
For mischief. Ants that straggle round their nest
His tunes are. That's the way he likes it done.
Why, if he meets me on a walk alone,
He strips me and leaves me flat—with twelve loose strings!

Aeschylus occupied half the play, comes forward with lyrics in which the words themselves seem to sing and dance, and there is expression for every tone of emotion and every new invention of contemporary music. And yet, at the end of it all, he has made tragedy a smaller thing! The poetry of Aeschylus weighs more.

It is mere blundering to say that Aristophanes thinks Euripides a bad poet and Aeschylus a good, or that he hates the one and loves the other. He sees that both are great poets; he admires both, loves both, but at the end of the count, old Aeschylus, with the glow of Marathon still upon him, Aeschylus who had triumphed with Miltiades and Aristîdes the Just, remains on his throne, shaken a little but not displaced. It is almost like comparing the regenerated Demos at the end of the *Knights* with the unregenerate Demos of Arginûsae; like comparing Aristîdes with Theramenes, the day of greatness with the day of downfall. And, apart from such associations, as a matter of pure art, the poetry of Aeschylus does really weigh more. He gives his vote for Aeschylus.

Yet, naturally enough, the verses that ran continually in his head, and seemed to weave about him a spell from which he had neither the power nor the desire to escape, were those of his own great contemporary.

CHAPTER VI

THE PLAYS OF ESCAPE
(*Birds*)

Most of the plays of Aristophanes are so strongly political, or at least so much inspired by public movements in contemporary Athenian life, that scholars when they treat of a play like the *Birds*, which on the face of it is as fanciful and as far removed from politics as *A Midsummer Night's Dream*, can hardly help asking themselves what it means, or—more prudently—what state of affairs in Athens formed the soil from which it sprang. It was produced at the Great Dionysia in the spring of 414 B.C. The great fleet which was to undertake the conquest of Sicily had set sail the previous summer, and had met so far with no great success or defeat. What was the feeling in Athens, or rather in those circles of the Athenian 'intelligentsia' to which Aristophanes belonged?

Some scholars have spoken of the 'dark shade of the fatal Sicilian expedition'; but that is to read into the spring of 414 B.C. the feelings of the winter of 413. The expedition had not yet failed. Others, like Mr. Rogers, consider that 'Athens was at the height of her power and prosperity' and that 'no shadow of the coming catastrophe dimmed the brightness of the outlook'. The first view would take the *Birds* as a reaction against despair, the second

represents it as an overflow of sanguine hopes and
high spirits. I doubt if either is quite satisfactory,
though I find more approach to truth in the first.

Let us cast our minds back to the Peace of
Nicias in 421, and to the idyllic comedy in which
Aristophanes welcomed it; the love-song of the
Cities escaped from death, ἄσμενοι ἐκ θανάτοιο—
dancing and laughing with their wounds and their
bandages. Cleon was dead, Brasidas was dead,
Athens and Sparta were friends, and the war that
had poisoned all the life of Hellas was now finished
for ever! Such expectations are seldom realized,
and certainly the years from 421 to 414 must have
been for Aristophanes a time of bitter disillusion.
The Peace, it may be said, was highly advan-
tageous to Athens. Possibly; but Aristophanes had
never urged the cause of peace simply because
Athens was not successful enough in war. He had
hated the war because it was war; because it meant
misery for all Greece and degradation and bruta-
lization for Athens. Seen from this point of
view the Peace of Nicias proved a rapid and ever-
growing disappointment. The agreements were
not fulfilled. Sparta's allies refused to sign. There
was a rapid outbreak of intrigues and military
alliances. Sparta and Athens were fighting each
other again in 418, and had only by accident
escaped doing so in 419. The savagery engen-
dered by the long war continued, and by the
winter of 416 reached its very climax in the

destruction of Mêlos by Athens, the massacre of its adult men and the enslavement of its women and children. The same thing had been done to Torônê in 422 and to Skiônê in 421. But these towns were rebels, reconquered in war; and the decree for their destruction was the work of the 'most violent of the citizens', Cleon. Even so, their fate had caused the name of Athens to be hated throughout Greece. Mêlos was a neutral, and was attacked for purely political reasons, without even a pretence of justice, in time of peace.

We know how some of the great minds of Athens were affected by these events. Thucydides devotes to the Melian affair no less than twenty-two chapters of cold devastating analysis, and, though he is not the man to suggest in so many words an intervention of Providence for the punishment of sin, he proceeds forthwith: 'In the same winter the Athenians made ready the expedition against Sicily.' Euripides wrote his *Trojan Women*, the greatest denunciation of war in ancient literature, and never.again was at peace with his native land. Aristophanes, who hated the war and the effects of the war even more openly and consistently than any of them, took these things differently. He turned away from the realities of public life. He had said what he thought of them in the *Acharnians* and the *Knights*; now, when they were worse, he preferred not to speak of them, and began to write about Utopias.

The first sign of this tendency is in the *Knights*
itself, when the Offal-monger heals old Demos of
his madness, rejuvenates him and makes him the
glorious being that he once was in the days of
Aristîdes the Just. The idea of Regeneration would
suggest itself easily from some of the commonest
rituals of ancient religion, in which the Old Year
with all its sicknesses and sins and pollutions was
cast away and the clean New Year welcomed in.[1]
That was the treatment which, in Aristophanes'
eyes, the world wanted.

It was probably soon after the Peace that he
wrote his *Gêras*, or *Old Age*, in which some of the
characters, and perhaps the Chorus too, throw off
their old age, as snakes slough their old skins. The
fragments chiefly suggest a sort of Kômos, like
that of Philocleon in the *Wasps*, but one may well
suspect that the rejuvenation had in it something
of the spirit of the *Knights*. One of the characters,
for example, remarks that his eyes were failing last
year, whereas now. . . . In the year 414 again, at
the Lenaea, a few months earlier than the *Birds*, he
produced the *Amphiarâus*, in which a 'very superstitious' Old Man, in bad health, goes with his wife
to the oracle of that hero and is enabled to recover
his youth. Bergk and Theodor Kock, on different
grounds from mine, have already suggested that
the Old Man is the Demos of Athens. The fragments remind one of the scene in the *Plutus*, where

---

[1] See Cornford, *Origin of Attic Comedy*, pp. 87–93.

the hero is cured of his blindness in the temple of
Asclepios. We find in them a mention of the
goddess of healing, Iâso, Amphiarâus' daughter;
of two patients listening eagerly for any sound,
and hearing a hen knock over a mug; of sacred
snakes; of a sort of exercise for making the back
supple during the process of rejuvenation; and we
have the curious line:

I know that what I am doing is old, and do not
deceive myself.

Perhaps he was apologizing for this old stage
motive of Rejuvenation, which he had used several
times before.[1] Later on, as we shall see, Aristophanes' Utopia takes other and different shapes: the
women unite to stop the war; the women unite to set
up a happy communist republic; the blind god,
Wealth, gets his eyes again and distinguishes the
good from the bad. But at the Dionysia of 414
B.C. the poet finds his heaven among the birds.

To touch for a moment on the actual situation
in Athens, it was a time both of trouble and of
Hubris. Mêlos had fallen in the winter of 416–
415. At the same time the vast project was formed
and debated of sending an overwhelming armada,
such as no Greek city could withstand, against

---

[1] The Utopia motive was common in Comedy; sometimes it came
through a Resurrection as in the *Frogs* and Pherecrates' *Krapataloi* and
Eupolis' *Demoi*: sometimes it was a Golden Age, as in Cratinus's *Plotoi*,
Crates' *Theria*, Pherecrates' *Metalles*; sometimes an escape from
civilization, as in Phrynichus' *Monotropos* or Pherecrates' *Agrioi*, where
the happy savages have no slaves.

Syracuse. If Syracuse were conquered all Sicily would become subject to Athens; and if Sicily fell, how could Carthage resist? What a vista then revealed itself! This scheme was enthusiastically urged by Alcibiades and vainly opposed by Nicias. Thucydides regarded it as an act of madness due to the folly of an excited populace and corrupt demagogues. Just before the fleet sailed, however, there occurred an extraordinary outrage, the history of which throws much light on the psychology of the Athenian mob. It was usual to have in front of the more important buildings a 'herm' or boundary pillar with two human characteristics: a bearded head, making the herm into the god Hermes, and a *phallus erectus* as an emblem of generation and fertility. On a single night, just before the fleet was to sail, all these images, except one that accidentally escaped, had their noses and phalli knocked off and were left mutilated. It is at first sight difficult for us to understand either the motives that led to the outrage, or the extraordinary state of public fury that it caused.

To the ordinary man in ordinary times such figures would, of course, be taken for granted and cause neither scandal nor enthusiasm. But the mutilation of them at a moment of extreme crisis, when it was of the first importance to have all the omens favourable, might well make a terrible impression. It would not merely be a crime against

the gods which cried for punishment; it would
actually have the effect of depriving a powerful god of his power to help. Such monstrous
malignity, the people would feel, must have some
abnormal motive behind it, some wish to paralyse
and ruin Athens. It must be the work of oligarchs,
of would-be tyrants, or traitors, or else of some
deliberate enemies of the gods.

In reality, perhaps, the motives were not so
abnormal after all. There must have been among
the more intellectual circles of Athens many who
had sat at the feet of Protagoras and Anaxagoras
and Socrates and whose ideas of God were utterly
unlike such foolish idols. Then, outside philosophical circles, there were men who had travelled
and knew how these phallic figures made the
Greeks ridiculous in the eyes of foreigners. More
important still, every serious critic of Greek civilization must have seen what a paralysing effect
was produced on public action by the innumerable
superstitions and scruples of the populace. A
wrong tinge in the victim's liver had more than
once wrecked a Spartan campaign: soon after this
a whole Athenian army was to be lost because of
an eclipse of the moon. We can appreciate the
strength of such terrors, and the repulsion which
they inspired among the intelligent, from Theo-
phrastus's picture of the 'Superstitious Man' and
from the enthusiastic reception of Epicurus's doctrine of deliverance. At this particular moment

Lysias tells the Athenians of a society called the Κακοδαιμονισταί, like the 'Hellfire Clubs' of the eighteenth century, which deliberately met and dined on forbidden days (ἀποφράδες ἡμέραι) and in other ways 'showed their contempt for our gods and customs'. There were men who occasionally parodied the Eleusinian Mysteries, which in many ways must have been tempting to parody. A generation later the pious Euthyphro in Plato's dialogue mentions that when he speaks in the Assembly about oracles foretelling the future, people laugh and think him cracked. A reasonable free-thought was no doubt spreading steadily during the fifth century throughout the educated classes, and writers like Thucydides and Aristophanes had risen well above the level of that εὐηθεία ἠλίθιος or *Ur-Dummheit* which still lurked in the traditional religion.

At this particular moment, however, public feeling took fright. Unscrupulous or ignorant demagogues lashed it to fury. A number of people believed to be guilty of the mutilation were put to death, others fled the country. The enemies of Alcibiades accused him but would not consent to hold an immediate trial. They let him start for Sicily but afterwards had him pursued and arrested, not for mutilating the Hermae—which was the last thing he was likely to do on the eve of his own great adventure—but for some alleged profanation of the Mysteries. And the armada set sail, in spite of all previous oracles and omens, under the shadow of an awful apprehension.

In this situation Aristophanes produced the *Birds*. His hero, Peithetairos, or 'Winfriend'[1] and his companion, Euelpides, 'Hopefulson', are utterly sick of Athens, sick of the high prices, the burden of debt, the everlasting informers, the ferocious law-courts, and the whole cloud of anxiety. It was in this year that Euripides represented his hero Ion as refusing to accept a princely fortune in Athens because he will not live in a city 'filled with fear' (φόβου πλέα, *Ion* 601). The two friends want advice about some place where one can live in peace, and can think of no better adviser than King Têreus, who was once married to an Athenian princess, and then was turned into a bird, the Hoopoe, and must by now have flown all over the world. Guided by a crow and a jackdaw they find Têreus, looking odd, but not odder than he was described in Sophocles' tragedy, and Euelpides explains what he and his friend want. 'There is', says the Hoopoe, 'a place that might suit you on the shores of the Red Sea'. . . . 'No. Not by the sea. An official ship from Athens might come and arrest us.' (Like Alcibiades.) 'There is Lepreon

[1] The MSS. gives the name Πεισθέταιρος, which is a false form and does not make sense. The easiest correction is Πισθέταιρος, 'Trusty-friend', but that does not particularly suit the character. He shows no particular 'trustiness' but great power of persuading or winning other people to his projects. Hence either Πειθέταιρος or Πεισέταιρος is probably right.

in Elis' . . . where the Spartans had just founded a colony of Helots who had fought under Brasidas! 'There is the region of Opûs in Locris' . . . where the population was particularly hostile to Athens and the Athenians had deposited a military post to control them! None of these is attractive. 'But what is it like here among the birds?' 'Not bad. You don't need a purse; and you find plenty to eat in the gardens.' At this point Peithetairos, hitherto silent, interrupts with a great shout. He sees a magnificent possibility. Let the birds unite and found one great city; let them put a wall round the air! Then they can rule mankind as if they were locusts, and master the gods by controlling their food-supply—which consists of course in the steam of sacrifices from the earth. The Hoopoe explodes in delight and admiration. He calls his wife, the Nightingale, from the thicket (their domestic differences seem to be forgotten, and her song is represented by a flute), and the two summon a grand gathering of the birds. The chirruping song of the Hoopoe is lovely, and presently the air is thick with 'long-throated birds', οἰωνῶν τανασλείρων, and loud with their musical cries. The number of birds known is remarkable. A flamingo comes first; then a cormorant and other individual birds which give a chance for jests at the fat Cleônymus and others of Aristophanes' special butts; then comes the whole army: halcyon, widgeon, francolin,

Jay and turtle, lark and sedge-bird, thyme-finch, ring-
dove first, and then
Rock-dove, stock-dove, cuckoo, falcon, fiery-crest and
willow-wren,
Lammergeyer, porphyrion, kestrel, waxwing, nuthatch,
waterhen.   (Rogers.)

'Why are they summoned?' they ask the Hoopoe.
'To speak to two men here. . . .' 'Men?' they
scream in horror. 'Men, our bitterest and wicked-
est enemies! Are you mad? Where are they that
we may peck their eyes out?' There follows a sort
of battle dance, in which the two men arm themselves with pots, saucers, and spits, rather like
Tweedledum and Tweedledee, until at last the
Hoopoe succeeds in inducing the Birds to listen
to reason.

Peithetairos expounds the ancient rights of the
Birds. They were once kings, a claim which he
illustrates by many examples; and now he can
show them how to recover their kingdom. The
Birds listen spell-bound. They are melted to tears
by his description of the way in which they are
now treated, pelted like madmen, driven out of the
temples where others have sanctuary, snared,
limed, caged, eaten and, as if that was not enough,
drowned in thick sauces! He shows in detail how
they can make or mar mankind; how they can
rule much better than the gods who have usurped
their throne. The Birds are wild with enthusiasm
and accept the plan. The two men are taken into

the Hoopoe's dwelling in the rock to be provided with wings.

The Birds left alone break suddenly into a lyrical summons to the Nightingale:

ὦ φίλη, ὦ ξουθή,
ὦ φίλτατον ὀρνέων . . .
ἦλθες, ἦλθες, ὤφθης.

'Dear one, tawny-throat, best-beloved of birds . . . you have come, you have come, we have seen you.'

Her fluting is to lead their song, which then begins in long anapaests. It is a great cosmogony in the style of Orpheus or Musaeus, addressed by 'the Birds of the Sky, who live for ever, ageless and deathless, and filled with immortal thoughts, to the dimly existing tribes of men, little-doing, moulded of clay, strengthless multitudes that fade as the leaf.'

Ἄγε Δὴ φύσιν ἄνΔρες ἀμαυρόβιοι, φύλλων γενεᾷ προσόμοιοι,
ὀλιγοΔρανέες, πλάσματα πηλοῦ, σκιοειΔέα φῦλ᾽ ἀμενηνά.

.   .   .   .

πρόσχετε τὸν νοῦν τοῖς ἀθανάτοις ἡμῖν, τοῖς αἰὲν ἐοῦσιν,
τοῖς αἰθερίοις, τοῖσιν ἀγήρῳς, τοῖς ἄφθιτα μηΔομένοισιν.

These birds, like Keats's nightingale, were 'not born for death'; no hungry generations trod them down, such as were now harassing Athens. They explain how in the beginning of things the Birds were born of Erôs and Chaos, how they are older than the Olympian gods, how in spite of their dethronement they still guide and direct human life, and how all signs and omens are 'birds'. Later in the parabasis they explain how their City will be an asylum for the misfits of the world; for father-beaters—since birds freely fight their fathers —for fugitives, for slaves and outcasts and barbarians, and for all, one might say, who are ashamed or unhappy among men. Then they expatiate on the usefulness of wings, chiefly for getting out of the theatre if you are bored or have other business, but also for climbing in the world, like Dieitrephes, the basket-seller, on his wings of wicker.

As often in Aristophanes, there is here a rush of real feeling and beauty, quickly apologized for and turned off with a laugh. And curiously enough, the feeling turns out to be based on something more than mere fancy; for the birds, as objects of worship in the Aegean area, were really older than the Olympian gods. Their sanctity goes back to pre-Hellenic times. Birds were in Greece, bringing thunder and rain, or giving signs to prophets, long before the anthropomorphic band of warlike Olympians descended from the northern forests: the eagle and the swan before Zeus, the owl before Athena, the dove before Aphrodite. There must have been more relics of pre-Hellenic cults extant in Aristophanes' time than we generally realize; but none the less it was a remarkable feat of imaginative guess-work, aided perhaps by some special love of birds in themselves, that enabled Aristophanes to catch this glimpse of a truth so long hidden from the generations after him.

Re-enter Peithetairos and Euelpides in their new wings, and in high spirits. What shall the city's name be? 'Nephelokokkûgia', suggests Peithetairos, a name which seems at first sight to be simply 'Cloud-cuckoo-land', but, since there seems to have been a wind called κοκκυγίας,[1] may carry a connotation embracing winds as well as clouds and cuckoos. Euelpides is sent off to help in the building and is not seen again. Peithetairos begins a solemn inaugural sacrifice, but the priest, who appears with a long prayer to the birds, parodied from Athenian ritual, at last calls so many birds that Peithetairos sees there will not be nearly enough for them to eat. He drives the Priest off, and is starting the sacrifice himself, when he is interrupted by an anonymous poet bringing a hymn in honour of the city and its founder ready-made, together with a lyrical request for baksheesh. This does not seem promising, but the man's verses are of the old severe school like Pindar or Simonides, so he has to be treated well. He is provided with the Priest's jerkin, but is still cold, and not contented till he has his tunic as well. Peithetairos begins afresh when in there bursts a χρησμολόγος, or collector of oracles, with some momentous revelations, among them a divine

---

[1] κοκκυγίαν· ἄνεμον οἱ Κροτωνιᾶται Hesychius (Schmidt: ἀνέμων ἢ cod.).

command that the first holy man to arrive shall
receive a cloak and new shoes. Peithetairos, however, happens to have another oracle strictly enjoin-
ing that the first religious impostor shall receive
a stick between the ribs, and the oracle-monger
vanishes. He is followed—rather to our surprise—
by Metôn, the great astronomer and reformer of the
calendar, who is treated with similar disrespect;[1]
then by a supercilious and well-dressed Commissioner, sent by the Ecclesia to supervise the
ceremonies. 'Will he take his fees and go?' asks
Peithetairos. 'Of course he will. His time is
precious and he has a motion to propose at the
Assembly.' The 'fees' descend upon him and the
Commissioner flies, but before he is well away
there comes a man provided with books full of laws
and decrees which may be useful in the new City.
As Peithetairos drives off one of these nuisances
on one side the second returns on the other side,
and both threaten him with legal proceedings for
assault, for *lèse-majesté*, for impiety, and for sacrilege, till he proceeds to extremities, and gives up
for the time being the attempt to sacrifice in the
open air. He goes indoors.

After another chorus about the help which the
Birds can give to man, a curse on Philocrates
the bird-seller, and a description of the happy life
of birds in the summer, when the grasshopper,

―――――――――

[1] Metôn's waterworks seem to be mentioned with respect by
Phrynichus, fr. 21.

'maddened with the sunshine and the rapture of the noon', sings below them, a Messenger announces to Peithetairos that the City wall is now built; but the description of it is barely finished when there comes news of a trespasser—some profane mocker who leaps over new walls, like Remus. Out goes a regiment of ten thousand falcons to arrest him. The guards presently return with a surprising prisoner—Iris, the rainbow messenger of Zeus, who is on her way to mankind to inquire why the sacrifices have stopped. Peithetairos affects extreme indignation. By what gates did she enter? Has she a passport? Have the ornitharchs given her a permit? Iris is bewildered. 'What is all this about permits and passports and ornitharchs? She is bearing a message from the Olympian Gods. . . .' 'Olympian Gods indeed! We are the Gods now, we Birds, and so you can tell your Olympians.' His bullying increases to such a point that the poor young goddess bursts into tears, and flies away to complain to her father.

Then comes the Herald back from the earth, where the revolution has been accepted with enthusiasm. Mankind, who used to be Sparta-mad, are now Bird-mad. Instead of going 'long-haired, unwashed and half-starved, like Socrates', they rise at dawn and fly to the νόμος—law, or, with a change of accent, meadow—they settle on τὰ βιβλία—books or papyrus beds—and fill their crops with ψηφίσματα—decrees or pebbles. Above all, they are clamouring for wings and are coming in crowds to get them. Instantly baskets and baskets of wings are brought, and there is some farcical business which cannot now be followed about the mistakes of the slaves in bringing them. They are only just in time, when in comes a Πατραλοίας, or Father-beater, clamouring to be made an eagle 'and fly over the unharvested sea'.

A father-beater is not, of course, a parricide, though he might become one: he is a 'bright young thing' who shows what he thinks of that iron parental discipline which was almost a religion in antiquity, by thrashing those who try to exercise it. We have had a case already in the *Clouds* (1320–1443). This *Patraloias* is treated with far more consideration than the prophets and the statute-mongers. He has come to the Birds because all young cocks fight their fathers. 'Yes,' says Peithetairos, 'but our law is also that of the storks. The young storks always feed their father.' This is a blow to the *Patraloias*; he has had his journey for nothing! The Birds are a fraud! 'Not quite,' says Peithetairos. 'Let your father be. We will fit you out as a soldier's orphan, with wing, crest and spur: now, off to Thrace with you, if you want fighting, and defend it against the barbarians!' The orphans of men slain in war were provided by the Athenian State with shield, helmet, and spear; and Aristophanes feels that the average rowdy half-criminal youth who during the long war had become a pest in Athens, had at least some stuff in him and might be a good man on the frontiers; which the other visitors in this scene could never be.

The next is a rather important historical character, Kinêsias, the most famous of Athenian lyric poets. One of his victories is recorded in an extant inscription (*I.G.* ii. 1253). He is condemned by Plato (*Gorg.* 502a) as one whose art aims only at producing pleasure, not good; in this he followed his father, Melês, 'who, however, while aiming at pleasure produced only boredom.' The lyrics with which he enters now, delightful as they are, show what Plato meant. They are all ethereal gleams and clouds and wings and snowflakes, rather like some of the prettiest songs in Euripides' *Helena.* We shall have more to say about this interesting person later on; here it is only his verses that come into question. The air, he explains, is his true home:

> Our dithyrambs' best beauties are but schemes
> Of mist and light and dark and cloudy gleams
> And fast wing-beating.

And Peithetairos proceeds to 'fast-wing-beat' him off the stage, rebuffed but still determined to be a winged thing and 'peragrate the air'.

In his place comes another singer, threadbare and sinister and badly in need of wings. He is an informer who makes a special business of serving writs on rich people in the islands. 'A charming trade! I congratulate you', says Peithetairos. 'Can't you dig?' 'No, never learnt.' 'Can't you do anything honest?' 'Come, no preaching. I want wings; wings, for business purposes. It is beautifully simple. I will fly to the island, serve the writ, fly back to Athens, bring on the case, get the islander condemned *in absentia* and there you are! I will spin there and back like a top.' 'Just so,' says Peithetairos, 'I'll make you spin', and whips him off yelling.

Returning he discovers a new arrival, of different type; a mysterious person so swathed in cloaks and veils that he can neither see nor be seen, nor even hear properly. 'Who are you?' 'Is any god following me?' 'No, but who are you?' 'What time is it?' 'Early afternoon. Who are you?' 'Closing time or later?' 'Oh, you make me sick!' 'Thank you. Is it cloudy or clear?' 'Confound you, stupid!' 'Thanks, in that case, I'll unroll.' He unrolls. 'My dear Prometheus!' cries Peithetairos, for it is indeed that friend of man and enemy of Zeus. 'Don't speak my name,' he exclaims; 'and please hold this umbrella over me, lest Zeus should see!' Prometheus has come to betray the secrets of Olympus. There is famine among the Gods; the barbarian gods up north are already starving and threatening to invade. Ambassadors will soon come, but Peithetairos will be wise to make no terms unless, first, the sceptre is given back to the Birds, and secondly, he has the beautiful

Basileia (Sovereignty) to wife. The umbrella duly returned to him, Prometheus departs.

Peithetairos promptly sets to work on the preparation of a tempting feast, and after a short Chorus the Embassy arrives. It consists of Poseidon, the old aristocratic god, patron of the Athenian Knights; Heracles, the strong beefy youth with more appetites than brains; and an absurd figure who proves to be a representative of the barbarian gods, a Triballian. He cannot understand or make himself understood, but he responds more or less to threats and blows from Heracles. 'Oh, Democracy!' sighs Poseidon, regarding him. Poseidon proposes terms of peace, but Heracles has his eyes glued on the cookery. (It consists, by the way, of some oligarchic birds who were condemned to death for conspiring against the State.) Peithetairos demands the restoration of the sceptre. The Birds will watch over men and see that they perform their oaths both to Birds and to Gods. Heracles eagerly agrees; the Triballian jabbers unintelligibly, but when Heracles asks him if he wants a hiding he apparently says yes. Poseidon is reluctantly giving way, when Peithetairos mentions as a slight extra that he also wants Basileia for his own. This Poseidon definitely refuses. Heracles hesitates. Poseidon appeals to him not to give up his whole inheritance, but Peithetairos whispers in his ear that he is not the heir of Zeus at all, being illegitimate, so that Heracles, left angry

and confused about the point of law, but indubit-
ably anxious for his dinner, consents. Everything
now depends on the Triballian. He jabbers at
some length, and the majority decide that he has
consented; so Poseidon is outvoted and Peithetairos has his desire. After another short chorus we
have his triumphal Kômos. The royal bride,
Basileia, is brought to him; surrounded by his
faithful Birds he dances with her his wedding
dance, he discharges the lightning and the thunder,
and is hailed as Kallinîkos, the Victorious, the
Highest of the Gods!

Δαιμόνων ὑπέρτατε: actually 'Highest of the Gods'.
One would have thought such words impossible. Greek doctrine is full of the punishments
of those who make themselves equal to even the
lowest orders of the gods, yet Peithetairos dances
off in triumph. We cannot tell how the audience
felt about it. The fact that the *Birds*, which we
moderns mostly consider the poet's masterpiece,
only obtained a second prize does not take us far,
for there are many ways in which the play may
have failed to catch the taste of the public.

But it does seem strange that the poet should
have had this successful pursuit of a great kingdom
in the clouds staged just at the time when, as
Thucydides and Plutarch tell us, Athens was
going mad after a kingdom in the west almost as
cloudy, and yet should have intended no particular
political reference. Nevertheless it is impossible

to discover any direct allusion, or even any clear attitude towards the schemes for the conquest of Sicily and Carthage. It cannot be an intentional encouragement of them, yet on the other hand it does not read like satire. It seems to be just an 'escape' from worry and the sordidness of life, away into the land of sky and clouds and poetry. If people want a cloud empire, here is a better one!

It was, we are told, in the previous year that Syracosios had brought forward his proposal for the prohibition of personal attacks in comedy. If so, the decree was either never passed or never really operative, for the personal references in the *Birds* are, if anything, more numerous, though on the whole lighter and less severe, than in the earlier plays. Most of them are concerned with literature; at least eleven poets or musicians come in for some chaff. With them may go the prophets Lampon and Diopeithes; the boasters, like Theogenes and Aeschines, and the many obscure persons who are likened in passing to some bird or other. There is mostly a careful avoidance of controversial politics: two cautious references to Nicias, one to Alcibiades, none to the warlike Lamachus—whom Aristophanes had attacked in the *Acharnians* and was to praise so handsomely after his death. Cleon dead and Hyperbolus ostracized are both now outside the picture; Euripides is not mentioned. But with all this reticence the old champion cannot keep his hands off some people.

They are mostly of the same type, cruel war-mongers, informers, and traders on the superstition of the public.

There is Cleônymus, usually compared to Falstaff, but really a much more sinister figure; one of Cleon's jackals (κόλακες), an informer, an oppressor of the Allies. It was he who moved in 425-424 B.C. the doubling and in some cases the trebling of the tribute; it was he who proposed a reward of a thousand drachmae for information about the mutilation of the Hermae and joined his ally Peisandros in inflaming the fury of the frightened mob. For these things Aristophanes must have hated him, but they hardly afford matter for good jokes. In the two earliest plays, the *Acharnians* and the *Knights*, Cleônymus was just a low hanger-on of Cleon's, very poor, very dirty, and with an enormous appetite (*Ach.* 844; *Kn.* 958, 1292 ff.). But from the satirist's point of view he improved. He became excessively fat; in war his belly betrayed him; and gods and men had laughed to see him running from the battle of Delium (424 B.C.) with his shield flung away. From the *Clouds* (423 B.C.) onward there is little mercy for the 'big Jackalonymus shedder-of-shields', the professional 'Never-betray-you' of the mob. A slave in the *Peace* dreams of an eagle seizing an Aspis—the word means both asp and shield—which it bore high into the air and then . . . then Cleônymus threw it away! In the *Birds* the Chorus tell of a strange tree in the land where there are no hearts; it is not exactly useful for anything, but still it is large and greasy and timid; in the spring it bursts into a bloom of figs and falsehoods, and in the winter sheds its—shields! (1473 ff.)

A similar figure is Peisandros, also a great Jingo and a great fat man, like a stout Acharnian ass. In the *Babylonians* we hear of him stirring up war; Lysias the orator says he found the confusion of war convenient for stealing in. In the *Peace* Peisandros' 'crests and eyebrows' make all decent people sick. Like Cleônymus, however, he suffered from nerves at the sight of real fighting. Not only a comic writer, like Eupolis, mentions that he went all the way to Pactôlus and was still the worst coward in the army; but the sober Xenophon (*Symp.* ii. 14) wonders what would happen to him if he did a sword-dance, since he cannot look at a spear! He seems to have had some dealings with the Socratics, for the Chorus (1553 ff.) describe how in some shadowy land where Socrates the unwashed brings souls to light (ψυχαγωγεῖ) Peisandros had come looking for his ψυχή—the word means both 'soul' and 'courage'—which had absconded in his lifetime; how he sacrified a camel to recover it and how there appeared something that looked like a ψυχή (ghost) but it was only —a starved philosopher. In the storm against the Hermocopidae he outdid Cleônymus. Cleônymus had a reward of 1,000 drachmae offered, but

Peisandros had it raised to 10,000 and actually carried a resolution for the torturing of citizens to obtain evidence. First a violent demagogue, he joined the oligarchs and took part in the reign of terror of the Four Hundred, and fled with them to Deceleia (410 B.C.). A sinister and repulsive figure, a type of what Aristophanes loathed.

'There is nothing like wings. Why, Dieitrephes, whose wings were only made of wicker, got chosen first a tribe-commander, then a General commanding cavalry, and now does great things and is a . . . tawny Hippalector' (ξουθὸς ἱππαλεκτρυών). So we are told at v. 798. A hippalector is a mythical monster compounded of a horse and a fighting cock, used as a figure-head for ships. We hear again that the words of Dieitrephes can 'give people wings'; in v. 1442 he 'sets young men flying' with desire to join the cavalry. One gets a fairly clear impression of this strange man: 'the lunatic, the Cretan, barely of Attic race', as Plato Comicus calls him; one of 'three shameless wild beasts', as he is to Cratînus (Plato, *Heortai*, 31; Cratinus, *Chirônes*, fr. 233). Fierce and half-mad, he excited the young men to martial ardour. In that shocking affair in 413, when the savage Thracian mercenaries made the massacre at Mycalessus, killing all the children in the school, and were so suitably cut to pieces by the pursuing Boeotians, Dieitrephes was in command. Doubtless the Thracians had got out of hand: Dieitrephes can hardly have ordered such doings. We do not hear of any charges of dishonesty or blackmail against him. He was not a squalid criminal. And curiously enough, though we do not know how he died, Pausanias mentions a statue of him, pierced with many arrows, set up by public decree on the Acropolis.

Then there is that Kinêsias who was flapped out of Nephelokokkugia and left flying in the air. There was much more against him than his new-fangled verse and music. He had not yet committed his great crime of 400 B.C. when he proposed and carried a decree abolishing the chorus in Comedy; nor had Aristophanes yet perpetrated against him—or at least against his name—the unforgettable yet scarcely malignant insult of the *Lysistrata*.[1] But there were other things. He was accused of impiety. He had notoriously defiled a shrine of Hecatê, one of those humble domestic objects of superstition which provoked the scorn of the intellectuals. He was actually a member of the 'Hellfire Club', the Kakodaimonistae. He seems to have been anti-democratic. He was twice in the courts against Lysias, who says that he 'deserted his art of poetry and made money by turning informer'. An extant inscription contains the decree proposed by him in honour of Diony-

---

[1] The name is chosen for the *double entendre* κινεῖν-βινεῖν, but it was not a common name and must have suggested the well-known poet to the mind of the audience.

sius I of Syracuse. It is interesting to notice in Aristophanes the difference of tone between the mocking of the rival artist Kinêsias, whose style he dislikes, and his grim onslaughts on war-mongers and informers. Aristophanes genuinely hates corrupt politicians and demagogues; but there is always a twinkle of good-nature in his most mischievous onslaughts upon artists. A passing accusation of unnatural vice, based on a poet's treatment of anapaests or his absence of beard, would no doubt be taken by Agathon and others in the spirit in which it was meant.

Cleisthenes had no art to excuse him, but it is difficult at first blush to see why he should be pursued with such relentless ridicule. True, he wore no hair on his face, a Macedonian fashion which did not prevail in Athens till about the time of Aristotle, but that in itself was hardly a sufficient crime. Of course, it makes him 'like a woman'. When the Clouds see Cleônymus they become timid deer, when they see Cleisthenes they look like women. In the *Thesmophoriazusae* it is Cleisthenes who comes among the women, as one of themselves, to warn them of Euripides' plot. When Mnesilochus, after shaving, looks in the mirror he seems 'just like Cleisthenes'. In the *Birds* we are asked how things can be expected to go well with a city where Athena the Maiden stands in full armour and Cleisthenes holds a shuttle. In the *Acharnians* he is called ὁ Σιβυρτίου, the son (or pupil) of a famous trainer of athletes, and we cannot say whether this means that the beardless man was really a great athlete—which would make most of the jokes rather better—or just the reverse. But the clue to Aristophanes' hostility is not far to seek. We hear in the *Knights* that Cleisthenes was one of the 'beardless' orators in the Assembly (1373 f.). And Lysias definitely calls him an informer.

He is one of a gang of men who have made profit out of the city's misfortunes and caused the gravest public wrong. They have persuaded you to condemn men to death without trial. They have brought about many unjust confiscations, banishments and degradations from civic rights. For money they would always try to get the guilty acquitted in the courts and the innocent destroyed. (Lys. xxv. 25.)

No doubt there is exaggeration in the pleader's statement, but it gives us just the light that we needed on Cleisthenes' real activities. It was not the absence of beard that enraged Aristophanes. A sŷcophantês without a beard would be hated for his smooth cheeks, but a bearded one would be just as much hated for his shagginess.

Aristophanes is still the same man that he was in the *Babylonians*, except that some of his illusions have gone. He no longer hopes with the old confidence to achieve real peace, to restore good feeling between Athens and her subject Allies, to get politics once more into the hands of decent people or see King Demos clothed and in his right mind.

He talks but little politics. He lives in literature, in μουσική. Even in μουσική, of course, all is not well; the young people nowadays do not know and love the great old poetry as they ought, and as for some of these new musicians, the less said of them the better! But in the realm of the Muses he can forget the world, its fears and its poverty and its intrigues; he can find wings for men or at least for the souls of men; he can laugh again, and laugh not bitterly but happily, laugh with an intoxication of fun and wild fancy and beautiful words, with no more bitterness in his heart . . . except of course for war-mongers and informers and persecutors, plague take the lot of them!

CHAPTER VII

THE LAST EFFORT FOR PEACE
(*Lysistrata*)

THE *Lysistrata* was acted in the early spring of 411 B.C. (February?) and was therefore composed in the atmosphere of the previous year. The Sicilian catastrophe of 413 B.C. had filled the city with consternation, so Thucydides tells us. Athens had lost her army, her ships, and the flower of her youth; her treasure was nearly exhausted, and she looked in vain for new sources of strength. The allies one by one began to revolt and to join the Spartans: Euboea, Lesbos, Chios, Erythrae went over to the enemy, and afterwards Miletus and Rhodes. The Persian satrap Tissaphernes also had just made a military alliance with Sparta. Faced with this desperate situation, the Athenians were cool and resolute. They built up painfully a fleet of 100 ships and a fair army, and one by one began recapturing the revolted cities. Athens was not yet conquered; by 410 B.C. indeed she had regained the command of the sea; but the strain must have been terrible. The oligarchical government of the Four Hundred began proposing rather futile terms to Agis for a permanent peace, which of course was much harder to obtain in present conditions than it had been in 421 B.C. It was now that Aristophanes made one last half-farcical half-tragic appeal.

A strange idea came to him. The times were not normal. The strain of war and the heavy mortality seem to have produced that spirit of feverish licence and pleasure-seeking which often accompanies the shedding of much blood. London, Paris, Vienna and Berlin knew it in the late war. Historians have described its excesses in the French Revolution and in the plague of Naples, to take only two instances out of many. 'What sensible thing are we women capable of doing?' asks Cleonîkê in this play; 'we do nothing but sit about with our paint and lipsticks and transparent gowns and all the rest of it' (42 ff.). 'If this were a festival of Bacchus or Aphrodite, instead of a serious peace meeting', says Lysistrata, 'it would be impossible to squeeze through the crowd; but now there is nobody here!' Later on, when continence is required of them, they break down: when they do take the resolve, they soon begin to fall away from it. 'Our whole sex is a mass of lust' (ὡς παγκατάπυγον ἡμέτερον ἅπαν γένος), says Lysistrata in her wrath, though there is never any suggestion that men are better. It is taken for granted that they are not. It was the same, doubtless, with all Athens: the reaction from the strain and disappointment of the great war left a deep and lasting mark.

Aristophanes, heavy-hearted for once and almost bitter, has the thought that these very lusts might be made an instrument to save Athens.[1]

[1] The idea of women ruling the State seems to have been peculiar to

Let the women use the cosmetics and scents and transparent gowns and the like as means to get mastery over the men and compel them to stop the war! 'If they do not stop it', says Lysistrata (33 ff.), 'the alternative is clear—there will be no Peloponnesians left' ('I should not mind that', says her hearer), 'no Boeotians, and as for Athenians . . . but I say no more.'

Gradually the women gather. It has been difficult for them to come: one was attending to her husband, who was starting for the war; another to the servants; others doing various things to the children, washing, feeding, putting to sleep and the like (16–19). Lysistrata and her friend Cleonîkê are there first; then Myrrhinê, a little frivolous; then others; then at last Lampito from Sparta, brown with the sun and 'strong enough to choke an ox'. With her come women from the other enemy states, Corinth and Thebes. They have come together to hear Lysistrata's great secret plan for stopping the war, and are prepared to accept it whatever it is. They will do anything. They will gladly die or cut themselves in pieces if only the war can be stopped. At last Lysistrata— the name is a real Greek name and means 'Dismisser-of-armies'—explains her plan. Men cannot live without women; let the women refuse to have

Aristophanes among the Comic writers, unless by chance Pherecrates' *Tyrannis* dealt with a despotism of women. The latter had plays about individual women, real or imaginary, *Thalatta*, *Korianno*, and one Λῆροι (*Trinkets*) on female dress.

any intercourse with men until the war stops. There is a painful silence. Then a voice: 'I can't do it. Let the war go on.' 'Nor I; let the war go on.' 'Anything else you like, dear Lysistrata, but not that. There is nothing else like it.' The Spartan woman has not spoken. Lysistrata turns to her and beseeches her help. If they two stand together. . . . 'Difficult, by the Twin Gods,' says the Spartan in her strong Doric; 'but . . . all right! We must have peace.' The two strong wills are enough. The others follow and a great oath is taken. The women swear, not over a shield, like the heroes in the *Seven Against Thebes*, but over a great basin of wine—that beverage, one part wine, and three parts water, which was the Athenian woman's substitute for tea. Just as the ceremony ends, a loud *Ololûgê*, or Woman's cry of Joy, in the distance tells them that their colleagues, the Old Women, have seized the Acropolis.

There is a tension of feeling in the writing, and a closeness to tragedy in the circumstances, which would have been fatal to a Comedy if they had been consistently carried through. That would never do. The play must be a farce, and since the feast is a phallic festival, it follows that the style of joke is determined. The play is, of necessity, indecent and more than indecent. The *phallus erectus* is treated as a kind of symbol, standing for all the thwarted desires and expectations that would arise in men alienated from their womankind.

To resume the story: on hearing of the seizure of the Acropolis a Chorus of Old Men—tough Marathonian veterans of the sort that Aristophanes loves—arrive on the scene with wooden logs and fire to burn the women out, but are confronted by a Chorus of Old Women with pails of water, ready to defend their friends. After a quarrel in which the Old Men are drenched with water, there enters a Proboulos, or Commissioner, with four Scythian policemen, whom he orders to force the gates and arrest Lysistrata. She comes out to parley, and the Commissioner calls on a policeman to seize her forthwith. At this there appears another woman, and another and another and another, till the police are outnumbered. The Commissioner none the less insists on making an attack—the attack and defence forming a mimetic dance for the Chorus. Repulsed with loss, he consents to parley, and demands an explanation. 'Why have they seized the Acropolis?' Lysistrata explains. They want to get possession of the Treasure in the Parthenon, so that the war cannot be carried on, and the Women may save Athens . . . and you yourself. 'But I don't want to be saved!' cries the Commissioner. 'You will be, all the same.' 'But what have you women to do with war or peace?' 'I will tell you,' says Lysistrata, and proceeds to describe the previous state of things.

> You never allowed us to utter a sound,
> But you needn't imagine, for that,

That our thoughts were content. We watched what
    you did
  From the quiet rooms where we sat,
And perhaps we would hear of mistakes you had made
  In some first-class public affair.
Then, pain in my heart and a smile on my lips,
  I would ask with an innocent air,
'Did the peace-offer come to the Council to-day?
  And what was it settled to do?
And will the decree be inscribed on the stone?'
  'Be off! That's nothing to you,'
Said my husband. 'You just hold your tongue.' So
  I held it.
A WOMAN. I wouldn't have held mine!
COMMISSIONER.   You would!
  Or else you'd have used it for screaming, my lass!
LYSIS. I held it! I quite understood.
  Then later, perhaps, when a rumour arrived
    Of some still stupider act,
  I might ask: 'What made them, my love, do a thing
    Which seems so perfectly cracked?'
At once he looked up at me under his brows:
    'Attend to your spindle', he said,
'And remember that War is the business of men,
  Or you'll soon have a pain in your head.'
COMM. A thoroughly sensible husband you had!
LYSIS. Is it sensible, never to take
The advice of a friend, and never confess
  When you know you have made a mistake? . . .
Well, years went by, and we heard in the street,
  One day, two gossiping men;
'Not a fighting-man left in the place', said the first;
  'Not one', said the other. So then,

We saw it was up to the women, at last,
  To muster their forces and cope
With the plague that was ruining Hellas. Why wait?
  If we waited, what was there to hope? . . .

Up to this point there is no mistaking the underlying seriousness of Lysistrata's tone: then comes
the inevitable turn towards farce and even 'Knock-
about'.

So now, if you're ready to listen in turn,
  And accept the good counsel we give,
And stay perfectly silent, we'll save you perhaps,
  And, with all your faults, help you to live.
COMM. Our faults! *You*'ll save us, you? Nonsense, I say,
  And unbearable nonsense!
LYSIS.   Keep still!
COMM. Keep still and let you do the talking, you jade?
  Not I. Strike me dead if I will!
And you in a veil!
LYSIS.   Would a veil of your own
  At all help you? You've only to ask it.
If that's the objection, that's making you frown,
There; wrap it well over, and pull it well down,
And then you'll be silent! . . . And take as a crown
  On top, this elegant basket.

Veiled and 'with his head in a bag', the Commissioner is reduced to silence, while Lysistrata
announces her programme. If Erôs and Aphrodite give aid, her women will stop the war. First,
they will put an end to the men's foolish habit of
going to the market in armour, buying fish or
cabbage or figs with a spear and a Gorgon shield,

and terrifying the old women who keep the stalls.
Then the women will take up the whole tangle of
public affairs and treat it as they treat their balls
of wool: wash out the mere dirt, pick off the burrs,
smooth out the bits that get together in lumps, and
then unite all together—citizens, resident aliens,
foreigners who are friendly, and those Athenians
who have been disfranchised—in one general skein
of Good Will.

COMMISSIONER. It is really too much! With their balls
　　　　　　　　and their skeins
　　These creatures think themselves clever.
　You have nothing whatever to do with the War;
　　Just remember that!
LYSIS. 　　　　　　　Nothing whatever?
　Why, it falls upon us twice as hard. What about
　　The sons whom we bear in our pain
　And send to the armies?
COMM. 　　　　　　　Ah, no more of that;
　　Don't stir old sorrows again.
LYSIS. And then, at the time when youth is at brim,
　　In the crown and flower of our lives,
　We lie all alone, with our men at the wars.
　　And it's not so bad for the wives,
　But it's hard on the girls, sitting there in their rooms,
　　Growing older, day after day.
COMM. But, bless us, men also grow old!
LYSIS. 　　　　　　　Yes, of course,
　　But quite in a different way.
　The man who returns, though his hair may be grey,
　　Can at once get a maiden for mate.
　But a woman's hour is short; it is gone
　　As she grasps at it, just too late.

No one will come for her. There she must sit
   Taking omens, while twilight is falling!
COMM. (*complacently*). Come, a stout old man with a leg
   and an eye. . . .
LYSIS. (*exploding*). Oh, why don't you die? I can never
   think why!
There is not too much time with your coffin to buy,
And the honey-cake—I'll come and knead it.
ANOTHER.   I'll tie
The funeral ribbons all round you!
ANOTHER.   And I
Bring the gifts for the grave, some wet and some dry!
LYSIS. What more do you want? The boat waits for
   you; fly!
                 Bestir yourself! Charon is calling!

It is not easy to make out exactly all the elaborate
'business' that is intended here. Evidently Lysistrata loses all patience, and the poor Commissioner,
who had felt so young and bridegroom-like the
moment before, goes off, with funeral bands tied
round his body and funeral libations poured over
his head, to show his outraged person to the
authorities. There is a short choral Agôn, or
Strife, between the Old Men and the Old Women,
when Lysistrata returns in anxious thought. Her
troops, it seems, are of poor material. The women
have, apparently, been about five days in the
Acropolis, and some are beginning to desert. She
has caught three or four already, and now there
are others. One of them remembers that she has
left a lot of wool out where the moths will get

it, another is anxious about a silk robe, another expects her confinement and cannot stay on the Acropolis because she has been frightened by the sacred Snake! Lysistrata firmly turns them back, comforts them with an oracle, and locks them in. The two Choruses then tell stories at each other. 'There was once', say the men, 'a hero called Melanion, who hated women, and went to the wilderness to avoid them.' 'There was once', answer the women, 'a certain Timon in Athens, who hated men, because he saw what they were like', and so on. At last comes the first sign that the enemy is weakening! A man is seen drawing near. It is Kinêsias,[1] the husband of Myrrhinê, and it is obvious from his appearance why he has come. Lysistrata gives directions to Myrrhinê to lead him on, play with him, madden him and cheat him, and so leaves her. Myrrhinê in a scene of a hundred lines carries out her instructions more than adequately. Kinêsias is easily induced to promise that he will vote for peace, and to repeat his promise.[2] Myrrhinê slips back into the Acropolis and he is left planted. He has scarcely left the scene in lamentation when there appears a Herald from Sparta eager for a Peace Conference.

---

[1] There is nothing definitely to suggest that this husband of Myrrhinê is meant to be Kinêsias the lyric poet: e.g. he does not enter reciting lyrics, as the real Kinêsias does in the *Birds*.

[2] So the Scholiast took 951. Others think that βουλεύσομαι means 'I will see', and is an attempt to evade his promise. If so, he deserves what he gets.

Preliminaries are arranged. Meantime the two hostile Choruses look at each other. The Old Men still strongly disapprove of the Women's conduct, but the Old Women flatter them a little, and re-arrange their cloaks, which have fallen off; one man has got an insect in his eye and a woman gets it out for him and wipes his eye, and then—in spite of his protest—kisses him! After this they form one Chorus. We should expect a mocking song, attacking certain individuals, but Aristo-phanes makes his Chorus say simply that at a time like this they will not speak ill of any one. Recon-ciliation is what is needed, between parties in Athens itself, as well as between Athens and Sparta.

In the next scene we have the entrance of the Spartan Envoys; the Athenians meet them, but they cannot make terms without Lysistrata. She enters with an allegorical figure, Diallagê, or Reconciliation, who takes Athenian and Spartan by the hand and joins them together. Then Lysistrata speaks. She is a woman, but after all she can think, and she has learnt history and politics in the only way that was open to ordinary people at the time, by listening to the words of her father and her elders. She accuses both Spartans and Athenians of great sin, in forgetting their common religion, gods and altars, and tearing one another like enemies. Do the Spartans not remember how Athens sent Kimôn to help them when they were nearly overthrown by the Messenian Revolt and the earthquake which came at the same time? Do the Athenians not remember how the Spartans sent Cleomenes and delivered Athens from the tyrants? Now let them be reconciled.

'We agree,' say the Spartans; 'though of course we must have Pylos again.' 'Never!' begin the Athenians, when Lysistrata checks them. They ask then for other places in payment for Pylos; the Spartans say 'Not all those!' Lysistrata again intervenes and both agree that the details do not really matter. The Reconciliation is made. The Athenians join their wives, and the Spartans theirs, who seem in some unexplained way to be present —the Old Comedy did not stick at small points of that sort—and the whole concourse goes in to a great banquet . . . materials for which have been secretly saved up by the women out of their allowances. A public banquet was a difficult undertaking in 411 B.C. After a short Chorus the feasters come forth again. The Spartans have been charming; and as for us, says an Athenian, we are so much better all round when we are a little drunk! When sober, we are too clever. We pay no attention to what other people really say but concentrate on discovering their motives for not saying something which they have not said, so that we never can give a straightforward account of any negotiations! A Spartan sings in broad Doric and dances what seems to be a Spartan war-dance in honour of the great deeds done by Athens and Sparta alike against the Persian. There is a procession of Spartans and Athenians, each man with his wife, an Attic hymn, and finally a Spartan hymn ending in an appeal to Athena of the Bronzen House, τὰν πάμμαχον, 'the All-warrior' or 'All-daring'.

A curious ending to a Peace Play, if indeed it is the end; though the final note here is not so much a eulogy of the comfort and ease of Peace, such as we had in the *Peace* and the *Acharnians*, as an appeal to the two great Greek Cities, Athens and Sparta, to stand together against all enemies of Hellas instead of working for their own mutual destruction. But probably the last few lines of the comedy are lost.

The message of the play, in any case, is considerably different from that of the *Acharnians* or even the *Peace*. In the *Acharnians* the cry was 'I hate the Spartans as much as you, but this war is senseless and makes every one miserable. Get rid of the war-mongers and fire-brands, and let us return to our farms and enjoy ourselves.' In the *Peace* the chief fire-brands were dead: every city in Greece was sick of war—except some neutrals, who made money by it. One pull, all together, and they can cheat the Gods who wish to destroy them and the politicians and informers who thrive on their sufferings. In the *Lysistrata* things are so dark that it is no good blaming anybody. There is no word against the democrats or the oligarchs, the mob or the conspirators, or even against any individual. They have all done badly; let them say no more about it but hold together. Above all, let them be reconciled with the great and noble enemy, Sparta. The old alliance, the deeds of mutual help, the old songs and choric dances of Sparta, the old steadfast habit and the tradition of heroism are called to mind, and the Spartan ideal set up beside the Athenian. One almost wonders, considering how near Athens was to her final collapse, that Aristophanes should dare to take this tone of free equality towards the enemy. But after all no one knew yet how the war would end. Athens was showing marvellous energy, and had still some big victories to come. She was not yet forced to approach Sparta as a suppliant.

The Old Comedy never takes much trouble with its characters. That was left for Menander and the New Comedy. Aristophanes generally has one central figure, the *scurra senex*, the shrewd and witty Old Man, who mocks at the various shams and impostures that rule the day, while the minor figures are only types. In this play there is no *scurra senex*: Lysistrata herself takes his place. There are women with names, Cleonîkê, Myrrhinê, the Laconian Lampito, who shines out in one scene, and perhaps others: but, except for differences of dialect, it is often not possible for an editor to decide which one is speaking, or even

to keep their characters consistent throughout.
It seems to be Myrrhinê, for example, who says
that her husband has been away in Pylos for seven
months (104); yet it is her husband who turns up
at l. 845 with no mention of having been away
at all. The one consistent and well-characterized
human being in the play is Lysistrata. She has a
touch of the heroic. She dominates every group,
male or female, in which she finds herself. She
is fully in earnest, and ready for all emergencies.
When the plenipotentiaries from Athens and Sparta
are met, the Leader of the Chorus calls to her:

> Bravest of women, now for you!
> To-day be terrible and weak,
> Daring and timid, proud and meek,
> And ever with resources new!

She reminds one of Peithetairos in the *Birds*, that
convincing leader of desperate enterprises. It is
noteworthy, also, that her dignity is never com-
promised, the regular mark of respect which
Aristophanes pays to his best heroes. She is never
caught flinching or lying or wanting to drink;
she has no husband or lover of her own, or, if the
'wife of Lycon' is really she (270), that is all we
ever hear of Lycon. Her language is in dignity
well above the standard of the other characters.
The others, for example, often say innocent
things which have indecent double meanings,
but not Lysistrata. When she does use a coarse
phrase it is a brutal truth rather than a joke.

Indeed, Lysistrata herself, like the whole play, illustrates well that curious divided allegiance in the comedian's mind which we have noticed before. He cannot help admiring the thing he mocks at, or perhaps rather he selects for the object of his laughter the thing that secretly fascinates him: Socrates, who makes the conventional world seem hollow; Euripides, whose verse and ideas haunt his imagination; the women who genuinely and whole-heartedly want peace and who have at least not shown themselves so desperately deluded as the men.

The *Lysistrata* is from time to time produced on the modern stage. There have been performances in London, in Paris, in Boston, and in New York, and recently in Cambridge. People are perhaps fascinated by the idea of doing something which, in the foolish modern euphemism, is called 'daring'. But, apart from their various degrees of 'daringness', such performances achieve little. They lack the two things which make the *Lysistrata* not merely a tolerable but an inspiring work of art. They lack utterly the background of traditional ritual; a ritual to which fertility was the main object of desire, and the phallus the recognized symbol of fertility. Without that background the play becomes consciously obscene instead of simply taking the indecency in its stride. It is hard to think of a modern parallel. But I once knew an English family which had a house full of reproductions of Italian religious pictures, showing the martyrdoms of numerous saints, and brought to it a Chinese nurse. The nurse besought them to take away these pictures: no doubt it was highly desirable that wicked men should be punished, but these punishments were dreadful and the pictures kept her awake at night with fear. To Western Christians the martyrdoms were merely part of a familiar tradition and consequently in no way shocking; to the Chinese woman, unused to the tradition, they came as fresh suggestions and caused a violent shock. She would not hang such pictures on her walls unless she wished to gloat on tortures, nor would a modern author write such a play as the *Lysistrata* unless he wished to revel in τὰ φαλλικά.

The modern performances suffer also from a greater lack. The *Lysistrata* has behind it much suffering and a burning pity. Aristophanes had more than once risked his civic rights and even his life in his battle for peace, and is now making his last appeal. It is owing to this background of intense feeling that the *Lysistrata* becomes not exactly a great comedy, but a great play, making its appeal not to laughter alone but also to deeper things than laughter.

CHAPTER VIII

THE BEGINNING OF THE FOURTH CENTURY

(*Ecclesiazûsae*, ?392 B.C.)

WHEN Aristophanes produced the *Frogs* in the early spring of 405 B.C. he was at the very height of his powers; some twelve years later in the *Ecclesiazûsae* we seem to feel the work of an ageing or an overtired man. It is more than the normal degree of change that one expects between, say, 42 and 55 even by modern standards; when we think of the splendid vigour of Sophocles and Euripides when well over 70 this loss of energy in their lively contemporary strikes us the more. We must remember, however, that the years in question were a time of great suffering, a time which comprised the final surrender of Athens, the destruction of the Long Walls, and the collapse of the Empire; the bloody rule of the Thirty Tyrants; the return of the Demos under Thrasybûlus, bringing amnesty and a return to the rule of law, but certainly not much prosperity and not much enlightenment—witness the condemnation of Socrates. These years must have been full of discouragement and fear for Aristophanes and the other intellectuals of the fifth-century type who remained. We know nothing of his personal circumstances, what battles and campaigns he took part in, what personal dangers, illnesses, or even persecutions he may have endured. There do, indeed, seem to be traces of one political play, bold and outspoken, that he dared to write in or soon after 411 (fr. 549, 550 Kock). According to a probable conjecture, it was about Alcibiades, but curiously enough we cannot tell for certain which side it took. It called him *Triphalês*—thrice a Phales, Phales being the daemon presiding over τὰ φαλλικά. But did it mean to condemn Alcibiades as 'thrice-debauched', which is the most usual view, or, as seems to me more probable, to exalt him as thrice-charged with vigour and blessing? The fragments do not decide the point, but in the *Frogs*, at any rate, Aristophanes seems to approve the counsel of Aeschylus that, if there is in the City a young lion, it is best to let him have his way.

It was his last cast. It failed, like most of the others, and after 411 B.C. the political ardour of Aristophanes seems to have waned. For one thing the times were dangerous. Attacks on Cleophon, the more hysterical and less formidable inheritor of Cleon's war policy, seem to have still been safe. Aristophanes has four contemptuous references to him (*Frogs*, 678, 1504, 1532; *Thesm.* 805); Plato wrote a whole comedy against him. But it is worth noticing that, while the date of Plato's *Cleophon* is unknown, the attacks of Aristophanes were made in 411 B.C. and 405 B.C., periods when Cleophon's

power was at its weakest. We must also remember
that Aristophanes was by now a disillusioned man.
The old liberal democracy that he had hoped for
in the *Knights* and the *Peace* was no longer a
possibility. All Aristophanes can do is to plead
for the 'weaving of a fabric of common goodwill'
(*Lys.* 579–86) and for an amnesty which shall wipe
out offences and make 'all Athenians equal' once
more (*Frogs*, 688). This policy was favoured on
the whole by the oligarchs, or at least by the
cultivated classes, rather than by Cleophon, and
was put into force by the Decree of Patrocleides
in the later part of 405. Aristophanes was at least
true to his old message of Peace.

It is seldom that a change of century according
to one of our arbitrary eras happens to accord with
a real change in social history; but one can well say
that the *Ecclesiazûsae* and the *Plutus* both belong
to the fourth-century style of literature. The bold
speech, the personal attacks on statesmen, the old
characteristic Parabases are gone. The Chorus is
greatly reduced. We find at least twice in the
Ecclesiazûsae (729, 876) and six times in the
Plutus the mere note XOPOY with no words, just as
in the papyrus of Menander. The dance and song
were no longer the business of the poet. If we had
more of the Middle Comedy preserved we should
doubtless find it closer to Aristophanes than Menander was, but we know too little to speak with
any confidence. The Middle Comedy dealt much

in parody and in Utopias, and we happen to have preserved in Athenaeus many Middle Comedy descriptions of food. There is a touch of all these elements in the latest Aristophanic plays. The banquet in the *Ecclesiazûsae* in particular is famous for one particular dish (1169): that of which the first twelfth part is λοπαδοτεμαχο-.[1] But besides the treatment of the Chorus there are several innovations in the *Ecclesiazûsae* which actually point the way to Menander and his contemporaries. A character called Chremês appears here for the first time, and plays a useful secondary part, just as he does in play after play of the New Comedy and its Roman imitations.[2] Then the sceptic or shirker who appears at l. 746 and argues with Chremês, or some other loyal citizen, produces a dialogue of quite the New Comedy style, quiet, witty, cynical, epigrammatic and with none of the boisterousness of the fifth century. The same may be said of the brief dialogue between Praxagora and her husband at l. 520:

[1] Rogers translates : Plattero-filleto-mulletto-turboto-
           Cranio-morselo-pickleo-acido-
           Silphio-honeyo-poured on the topofo-
           Ouselo-throstleo-cushato-culvero-
           Cutleto-roastingo-marrowo-dippero-
           Leveret-syrupo-gibleto wings,
but the joke does not work in modern English. It might in Rabelais.

[2] The names Χρέμης, Χρέμυλος, Χρέμων, are real names: derivation uncertain. As used in Comedy they are probably meant to suggest 'coughing' or 'snorting'.—It is worth remarking that, while in tragedy the Θεράπων or Ἄγγελος remains nameless, in comedy the 'First Citizen' or 'Second Citizen' tends to become 'Chremes', 'Demeas' etc.

'You don't imagine I have come from a lover?'
'Perhaps more than one.'
'You can easily tell.'
'How?'
'Smell my hair.'
'Does a woman never go to a lover without scenting her hair?'
'I am sure *I* never would.'

This is markedly fourth- or third-century in tone: so is the charming misunderstanding where it seems that the Ecclesia ἄρρεν ἔτεκε παιδίον (549). There is real Aristophanic wit in the play here and there; but in the main the old fiery and turbulent vitality, which could carry off not only a political play like the *Knights*, but even a highly intellectual play, like the *Clouds* or the *Frogs*, seems by now to have died down.

Aristophanes had failed more than once because his comedy was too 'high-brow' for his audience, and seems to have been anxious in the *Ecclesiazûsae* not to do so again. He claims at the end of the play the suffrages of the intellectuals (σοφοί) for his new philosophic ideas, and those of all who love laughter (οἱ γελῶντες ἡδέως) for the laughter he has provided. Evidently he is anxious to combine the two. The Chorus urge Praxagora to give the audience 'ideas never practised and never suggested before' (μήτε δεδραμένα μήτ' εἰρημένα πω πρότερον, 579). They bid her 'awake a shrewd and philosophic mind' (πυκνὴν φρένα καὶ φιλόσοφον ἐγείρειν). She herself says that what she most fears is that the audience may not like new ideas or jokes, but prefer to stay in the old ruts (583 ff.). In the *Frogs* he pleased the *Sophoi* with his literary criticism and the 'low-brows' with lots of lively farce; here he seems to have rather lost his spring and to have tried to make up for it by somewhat obscene extravaganza. One can imagine him working up the joke about Blepyrus' nocturnal troubles, or the long scene with the Three Hags, and saying to himself, 'Surely, they cannot say it is too highbrow now!'

The philosophic ideas are certainly prominent, and the strange thing is that they all seem to be drawn from Plato's *Republic*, which at first sight seems flatly impossible. The play was produced not later than 391 B.C.—Rogers would make it 393—and the *Republic*, as we know it, cannot have been published till about twenty years later, some time shortly before Plato's voyage to Sicily in 367 B.C. The problem has been much discussed, but the true answer was indicated long ago by Bergk (*Literaturgeschichte*, iv, p. 86) and has been made clearer still by Jäger's work on the chronology of Aristotle's writings. The truth is that our conception of 'publication' does not fit ancient conditions. A modern book is written, set up in type, corrected, revised, and eventually printed off in hundreds of identical copies on a given date. Every copy of an ancient book had to be written out separately. An author might always read his manuscript to an audience before it was multiplied; a friend might get leave to read it or even to copy it; nay, in the case of a philosopher it might exist in the form of notes used for lectures many years before it was published as a finished work. Furthermore, a 'book' was a papyrus roll; the *Republic* consists of ten books, and it is not very likely that a work of ten books was either composed at one continuous effort or that each book was kept unseen and secret till all ten should be ready. The subject is obscure and needs study; but one of the cardinal facts which any satisfactory theory must explain is this knowledge by Aristophanes of certain daring paradoxes of Platonic thought long before they appeared in their present form in Book V of the *Republic*.

Of course it remains possible that the Platonic conceptions of Woman's Rights, Communism, and the abolition of marriage may have been 'in the air' at this time; or even, as Favorinus says, may have been suggested by Protagoras' *Antilogika*,[1] but Aristotle in discussing them attributes them only to Plato and says explicitly that the novel proposals about community of children and of women ... 'have been made by no other'—i.e. presumably, 'no other philosopher' (Ar. *Politics*, 1266a 34 ff.; cf. 1274b 9–11). And though of course the doctrines are caricatured, the enfranchisement of

---

[1] Diog. Laert. iii. 1, 57.

women being transformed into a disfranchisement of men, and the stern abnegation of self imposed upon Plato's Guardians into a loose and joyous communism and free Kômos of all citizens, the correspondences with Plato's language are too close to be accidental. Immediately after Praxagora has expressed her fear that these ideas may be too original for the audience she starts with Plato's key-word, Κοινωνία—Partnership or Community (590). The land and all movable property are to be common, as in Plato (*Rep.* iii. 416d). The women too, as in *Rep.* iv. 423e, v. 457c, d, 464b. 'How will a father be able to know his son?' asks Plato (*Rep.* v, 461c, d), and the same question in almost the same words is asked here and receives the same answer (635 ff). There will be no lawsuits, because there will be no frauds; no provisions for preventing assaults because there will be no assaults; the meals or feasts will be in common. Compare Plato, *Rep.* v. 464d, e, 458c. To my mind there can be little doubt of the connexion. Aristophanes seems clearly to have known some early form of the *Republic* and it is more than possible that Plato, in the passages where he refers to the ridicule which his ideas are likely to meet with, is referring to the *Ecclesiazûsae*. If so, a small question arises about ancient manners. There is every reason to believe that Aristophanes and Plato were friends; Plato makes Aristophanes one of the guests at the Symposium, and is stated by his ancient biographers to be the author of an epigram saying that the Graces, when looking for a temple that would never fall, or, as we should say, a garden that would never fade, found the soul of Aristophanes.[1] That being so, it is interesting to see how much public 'chaff', and within what limits, a friend could be expected to stand without offence. The standard seems to have been much the same as our own. The poet never mentions Plato by name, nor even gives the slightest hint that Praxagora's fantastic ideas come from any particular sophistic or new-fangled source. That would doubtless have been rude. On the other hand, he felt himself free not only to make great fun of Plato's doctrines, but to caricature them in order to make them funnier. It would, I think, be quite a mistake to regard the play as a serious criticism of ideas of which Aristophanes disapproved.[2]

The scene, as usual afterwards in the New Comedy, represents three houses. Praxagora,

---

[1]
Αἱ χάριτες, τέμενός τι λαβεῖν ὅπερ οὐχὶ πεσεῖται
ζητοῦσαι, ψυχὴν ηὗρον 'Αριστοφανοῦς.

[2] The relation of the *Ecclesiazûsae* to the *Republic* has been much discussed since the time of Lebeau in 1760: cf. especially Bergk, *Literaturgeschichte*, iv, p. 86; E. Meyer, *Geschichte*, iv, p. 429 (who has the odd notion that Aristophanes hated Socrates but liked Plato, and therefore did not caricature him); Kaehler, *De Ar. Ecclesiazusarum tempore et choro*, 1889; Adam, *Republic*, i, pp. 345–55, who gives a good account of the more recent literature; Zeller, *Plato*, p. 140 of Engl. trans. See also Geffcken, *Literaturgeschichte*, i, p. 255; also, of course, Rogers, p. xxii.

mistress of the centre one, is on the stage in dark-
ness with a lamp, wearing a man's tunic, cloak, and
shoes, and ready to take her place in the Ecclesia.
She is impatient that her fellow-conspirators do not
arrive. She speaks in verse of a metrical correct-
ness which is more like tragedy than comedy for
some thirty lines. She sees a masculine figure
approaching and withdraws; but it is only the first
of her colleagues in disguise. She scratches lightly
on the door of one of the houses; and a third
woman comes out. Others arrive later. They are
not only wearing men's clothes. They have been
systematically, though secretly, sun-bathing to
brown their skins. They have encouraged hair to
grow on their bodies and one has 'thrown the
razor out of the house' (63–7). More than this,
they all have their beards either on or ready. They
begin to practise for the Assembly, but one unwisely
thinks of taking her spinning there. Another, who
is told to speak and is given a garland, misunderstands the garland and expects a drink. A third
starts well, but unfortunately uses a female ex-
pletive, μὰ τὼ θεώ ('By the two goddesses!'). At
last Praxagora herself begins a speech in the best
parliamentary manner, while the others practise
applauding—with only one bad mistake, an oath
'By Aphrodite!'—Praxagora dwells on the general
confusion and inconsistency of Athenian politics,
the class quarrels, and the lack of public spirit.
The only hope is to hand over the whole govern-

ment to the Women. Women do not chop and change. They keep all the good old customs. They still carry things on their heads, still keep the religious festivals, as they always did:

> Still cook things sitting, as they always did;
> Bake the old cheese-cakes as they always did;
> Hold down their husbands, as they always did:
> Have secret lovers, as they always had,
> And then they're happy—as they always were!

They will take motherly care of the soldiers. They are good economists and managers. They can always find money; and more—they cannot be cheated.

Her companions wonder at her power of speech. 'Where can she have learnt to speak so well?' She learnt it during the flight from the country early in the war, when she and her husband had to live in some shed on the Pnyx and could not help hearing the orators all day long.

Praxagora is appointed Stratêgos or Dictator, and after some further arrangements about getting front places in the Assembly and escaping detection, the women march off in two bands, the city women and those from the country. The stage, still dark, is for a moment empty when there enters a strange figure. This is Praxagora's husband, Blepyrus, who has unfortunately been seized with griping pains and on wishing to come out to relieve himself cannot find his clothes. There is nothing for it but to put on his wife's little shoes and saffron

silk gown. He is presently interrupted by a neighbour whose clothes—and whose wife—have disappeared in like manner. They wonder together,
and the neighbour goes off to the Ecclesia;
Blepyrus, not yet feeling well, remains. After a
due interval there enters one Chremês—already
perhaps, as noticed above, beginning to be a stock
character in Comedy—who has just come back
from the Ecclesia. It had been a funny meeting,
he says: the place quite crowded out, apparently
with shoemakers: pale small people with beards
who occupied all the front, so that he could hardly
find room. First the orator Neocleides spoke, to
no purpose, as usual; then a certain Euaiôn, who
seemed to want to receive charity. Then a smart
pale young man whom he did not know, but who
was cheered to the echo by all the shoemakers.
He spoke well, but ended by proposing that the
government should be handed over to the women!
He praised women, and said all sorts of things
against men like you. 'Why like me?' They were
rascals, thieves, informers. 'Only me?' 'Oh, all
these people too', says Chremês, indicating the
audience. 'Women can keep secrets, unlike men.
They lend each other things and return them—
unlike men—even when there is no witness. And
most unlike men, they don't inform or prosecute
or conspire!' Thanks to the shoemakers, the proposal was carried by a large majority, and there is
nothing more to be done about it. After all,

when Poseidon laid on Athens the curse that she should always make the wrong political decision, Athena had added the blessing that things should turn out well all the same! With this comforting reflection the two men go in at their respective doors.

Secretly and with extreme precaution the conspirators return and, finding they are alone, take off their beards and change their clothes. The Chorus, who presumably had already changed, remain. Praxagora is proceeding to enter her house when she meets her indignant husband. 'What mischief have you been up to?' 'Mischief, when I have no scent on my head? I have been to help a friend who was in labour.' 'And why did you take my cloak?' 'It was warmer than mine, and you were quite warm and comfortable, whereas I am thin and chilly.' 'And my shoes! And my stick!' 'Of course, I was afraid of slipping and spoiling your beautiful cloak.' 'Well, you have lost me the pay I should have got at the Ecclesia!' 'Never mind. It's a boy.' 'What's a boy? The Ecclesia?'[1] 'No, the baby. . . . But has there been an Ecclesia?' 'Yes, I told you yesterday.' 'Oh, I forgot. What did they do?' she asks with every air of innocence. Blepyrus tells her the news, which she receives with jubilation. 'Now all will be well! No more witnessing and informing!' (Blepyrus: 'Don't take away our

---

[1] *Pr.* μὴ φροντίσῃς· ἄρρεν γὰρ ἔτεκε παιδίον.
Bl. Ἡ Ἐκκλησία;   (549)

livelihood!' Chremês: 'Don't interrupt a lady, Sir!') 'No more thieving, starvation, wrangling, distraining. . . .' 'How do you make that out?' asks Blepyrus, and Praxagora in answer proceeds to a full exposition of the New Republic. There is to be, first of all, community of land and servants.[1] Women shall administer; all portable property shall be brought in to the common store.

BLEPYRUS. Suppose a man won't bring his?

PRAXAGORA. He will gain nothing.

BLEP. Suppose he wants to make private presents to a girl?

PRAX. Private love-making is swept away. There is community, *plus* trade union rules, to prevent any unfair advantage accruing to youth or beauty. The old and ugly of either sex must be protected and have the first right to a mate.

BLEP. But suppose they fight. . . .

PRAX. They won't fight about *you*, dear.

A number of obvious objections are made by Blepyrus. 'How will a man know his own children?' He will not: all elders must be treated with the respect due to fathers, all the young with the kindness due to sons and daughters. 'Who will work the fields?' The public slaves will do that. 'Who weave the clothes?' The women, of course. 'What about those who owe fines to the State, about debtors, about brawlers, thieves, garrotters,

---

[1] Slavery is not abolished, any more than in the *Republic*, where it is simply ignored except for the remark that a Greek should never be slave to a Greek. In the Ἄγριοι ('*Savages*') of Pherecrates there are no slaves in Utopia.

gamblers?' She has no difficulty in showing that
such things will cease to exist; at the worst, if a
man misbehaves his food can be docked. There
will be no private houses; the Bema and the Pnyx
will be used, not for silly politics as now, but for
concerts and recitations to encourage virtue. The
law-courts shall be turned into dining halls and
there shall be no more prostitutes. Life shall be
a perpetual merrymaking! Praxagora must repair
to the Agora to arrange for the reception of
property and the feasting, since she herself has
been elected chief magistrate.

The effect of this speech is entirely to convert
Chremês, and to make Blepyrus extremely proud
of being the 'husband of the Dictator'. There
follows a note in the text 'Chorus', but no words
are given. This is the first instance of a practice
which seems to have become regular in the New
Comedy. Its exact meaning is not certain, but it
seems most likely that in place of a lyric written
by a poet and performed by a Chorus of Athenian
citizens we begin to have simply an interlude of
some sort performed by professional dancers. The
demand for artistic skill, so to speak, is transferred
from the composer to the performers.

There follows an amusing scene between a loyal
adherent of the new order (perhaps Chremês),
who is collecting his household goods in a sort
of procession to go and be surrendered to the
public authority, and a sceptical onlooker who is

determined not to be such a fool. 'Nobody will do
it! The decree will never be carried out! Besides,
they are sure to change the law in a few days, as
they always do. Think how they changed about
the salt, about the copper coinage, about the tax
of 2½ per cent.' Before the dispute is finished, a
Female Herald (Κηρύκαινα) enters to proclaim the
great Communal Feast, to which all are invited
who have sent in their property. The Sceptic,
shaken, hurriedly offers to help Chremês to carry
his things in. Refused, he thinks of fetching his
own, but fears he is too late even now; he decides
to 'gate-crash' and trust to luck. On this there
follows another Chorus with no words attached.
Presumably there was a dance in which the gate-
crasher made his onslaught and met with the
treatment he deserved. There follows a scene
which has quite good comic material at the back,
but is somehow wrongly handled. Certainly it is
too long, and it ends, in the opinion of most
readers, by leaving an unpleasant impression. A
young woman and an old woman are waiting for
a young man who has, it would seem, an appoint-
ment with the former. The two wrangle with each
other. The Young Man comes, sings with the girl,
but is claimed and seized according to the new
law by the Old Woman. To his joy he is rescued
by the intervention of a third claimant, who, however, proves to 'be older and less attractive still;
struggling to get away from her he is rescued again

by a fantastically hideous and corpse-like Hag,
and disappears in danger of being torn in two by
the pair of them. It is a relief when he goes and
we have instead a Maidservant of Praxagora come
to summon the Dictator's husband and children
to the feast. Happy he, the only man in the city
who has not yet dined! The Chorus in a few
closing lines speak in the poet's name to the Five
Judges, thus taking on the functions of the old
and obsolete Parabasis. Let the lovers of philosophy
select him, let the lovers of laughter select him;
and let them not forget him because, by the casting
of the lot, his play has been acted first and others
will follow. The discussion of theoretic communism ought, he hopes, to be interesting to the
real high-brow lover of philosophy, if only it is
not too abstract for the average spectator. And
one seems to see the old poet, afraid that the play
is too philosophic, debarred from his old Chorus,
debarred again from his bold satire on public
affairs, conscientiously and heavy-handedly making up for these disadvantages by inserting the
indecent jokes. The play differs greatly from the
Lysistrata, first, in its lack of fire and intensity of
feeling, in the comparative lack of interest of its
theme, and in the marked inferiority of the heroine.
In the earlier plays Aristophanes may be, and
indeed is forced by the nature of the Dionysiac
festival to be, highly indecorous: but he is strong
in his feelings, swift and fiery in his high spirits,

splendid in his courage. In this play for the first time one feels a certain lingering quality in his obscenity which definitely belongs to the literature of fatigue, such as meets us in Rome just before and after the Christian era, or in Western Europe in the twentieth century.

CHAPTER IX

THE *PLUTUS* AND AFTER: ARISTO-PHANES AND THE ANCIENT CRITICS

EVERY man's last battle, says the Icelandic proverb, is a defeat, and in that defeat he can best show his true quality. Aristophanes came near to eluding this unescapable law. His own vitality waned, and he saw his great war-horse, the Old Comedy, killed under him, but before leaving the field he did, with remarkable originality, point the way which was to be followed after him by Greek Comedy, Roman Comedy, and, one may almost say, the whole theatre of modern Europe.

His last extant play is the *Plutus* (388 B.C.). It has been much praised, and was widely read in later antiquity. It exists in no less than 146 manuscripts. If true plays of the Old Comedy were not extant probably one would think very highly of it, but, compared with the *Birds* or *Frogs* or *Knights*, it is rather a bloodless performance, interesting chiefly for its place in the history of literature. It is written for an audience which could no longer quite stomach the Old Comedy, with its reckless language, its personal abuse, its concentration on great public issues, and its passionate idealism. The *Plutus* belongs to a time of great 'financial stringency', as we now call it; when Athens was too poor to afford a Comic Chorus, or even a State medical service, and to have really enough to eat was for most Athenians a rare and thrilling experience.

The opening is in the Old Comedy style. The slave Carion cannot any longer stand the absurd ways of his master, Chremylus, who continues to follow in the steps of an old blind and silent man in beggar's clothes. He insists on an explanation, and Chremylus explains how, being honest and poor, and seeing all round him the riches and prosperity that came to thieves and burglars, informers, politicians and other scoundrels, he had gone to ask Apollo's counsel, whether he would not do well to change his mode of life and grow rich; how Apollo had told him to follow the first person he met on leaving the temple, and how this blind man was he. 'Then let us at least find out who he is.' With great difficulty, by threats and promises, the blind man is induced to reveal himself. He is Plutus, the god of Wealth; Zeus had blinded him long ago, out of ill-will to the race of man, and now poor Wealth, unable to see where he is going, stumbles into the society of the most dreadful people, and is treated shockingly! Amazed at first, Chremylus soon sees what must be done. They must take the blind god to the Temple of Asclepios and have him cured. Wealth is terrified; Zeus will never forgive him if he attempts such a thing. ('Wealth is always cowardly', remarks Carion.) They persuade Wealth, however, that he does not realize his own value. It is through

him that people have power; it is for him that they
all exert themselves—and incidentally for his sake
that they sacrifice to Zeus. Wealth is the one
thing of which men never have enough; of all else
there comes satiety: Chremylus and Carion in
alternation enumerate the objects of desire and
satiety: men have enough

CH. Of love, CA. of bread, CH. of music, CA. nuts and
things,
CH. Of honour, CA. cheesecakes, CH. virtue, CA. figs
in strings,
CH. Ambition, CA. porridge, CH. glory, CA. lentil stew;
CH. But no man ever has enough of you!

Wealth at last agrees to risk it, and enters into
Chremylus' house.

Here we meet an interesting change from the
Old Comedy. Carion is sent to summon his
master's Συγγεωργοί, or Fellow-Husbandmen, who
would naturally form a proper Aristophanic chorus.
And so in a sense they do, but with a difference.
At their first entrance we seem to have two alternative versions. First comes a rather spirited Aristophanic lyric, if one can call it a lyric, in a very
unambitious metre: just the same iambic tetra-
meters catalectic as the preceding dialogue, with
occasional half-lines. Next comes a note, XOPOY,
such as we had in the *Ecclesiazûsae* and shall find
hereafter in the New Comedy. It would seem
that, if the producer was content with very simple
metres and the corresponding dance, Aristophanes

could provide songs suitable for an average Chorus of citizens; if he wanted a more elaborate and difficult performance, he must bring on a special chorus of professional dancers. Later in the play we have the note XOPOY half a dozen times, besides one place where it has been restored by editors though absent in the manuscripts.[1]

When Chremylus comes out again from his house (322), in which Wealth is now established and consequently all is opulent, with abundance of meal, wine, and oil, and all the vessels turning to gold and silver, we have a scene that smacks more of the New Comedy than the Old, though there was something like it in the *Ecclesiazûsae.* A neighbour of Chremylus, Blepsidêmus, pays a visit, and is much intrigued by his friend's sudden prosperity. There must be some explanation and he suspects the worst. 'Is it bribes? Is it burglary (τοιχωρυχία[2])? Is it peculation of public funds?' In any case he is willing for a suitable consideration to hush it up and bribe the orators to say nothing about it. Chremylus with difficulty convinces him of the truth and explains that he is going to heal the blind god's eyes. 'But there aren't any doctors now in Athens! The city couldn't afford them' (407 ff.). It is not a case for mere human doctors; they must go straight to Asclêpios.

---

[1] After 1170, Bergk. Once, after 770, it is Κομμάτιον Χοροῦ: meaning 'Short bit'?

[2] τοιχωρυχία, 'wall-digging'. The ancient burglar dug his way conveniently through the mud walls of a house.

At this moment (415) there bursts in a haggard young female of superhuman stature, like a Fury from a tragedy. Who can she be? 'From her looks,' says Chremylus, 'one would say she was an angry barmaid. Have you been cheating one lately?' In reality she is the goddess Poverty, the maker and saviour of Hellas, the mother of all strenuous effort, all virtue, come to warn them against the disastrous policy on which they are embarking. If they make every one rich all energy and industry and manliness will be lost. (In strict consistency they might have answered that they never proposed to make every one rich. On the contrary, if Wealth is made to see, he will live with the good and avoid the bad. The poet, however, ignores that subtlety.) The two men simply refuse to listen to this tale of the advantages of Poverty. It may all be true; they seem to have heard it before; but, anyhow, they don't believe a word of it, and Poverty may go and hang herself! They take up their bedding and proceed to the Temple of Asclepios, where they are to spend the night in the ritual of Incubation (620–6).

The night passes. Here again there must have been some interlude, or choric performance, after which Carion bursts in with joyful news. He summons Chremylus' wife from the house, and relates to her the whole story of the Incubation in the temple. This wife, I think, is the first comic female character in Greek literature. I mean, the first woman who is made funny not because of her sex, but because of her character. She is a nice ignorant pious Athenian *Hausfrau*; and half the fun of the brilliant scene in which Carion describes the Incubation comes from her reception of it. She is so credulous and so easily shocked. The patients were all put to bed in different parts of the temple, the offerings of food and drink laid on the altars, and some possets or 'nightcaps' apparently set out for the patients themselves. The lights were extinguished, and Carion saw a priest stealing round and 'consecrating' the best food into a bag. No doubt the god and his divine attendant would be supposed to have consumed it! Meantime Carion, hungry as always, had seen a large bowl of broth near the head of an old woman, and could not sleep for thinking of it. He was crawling silently in the dark towards it when the old woman moved; with great presence of mind, he hissed, like one of the sacred snakes, and delicately bit her, so she crept under the bedclothes 'like a frightened cat', and there stayed, while Carion ate till he could eat no more. Later on the God himself came round with two divine Maidens, touched the eyes of Wealth, and had them licked by the sacred snake; and now Wealth can see!

Presently Chremylus and Wealth himself return, Wealth gives thanks, and they go into the house. There is another pause and doubtless an interlude.

Then comes a series of visitors, like those in the

earlier plays, though described perhaps with less
spirit and more of what the Greek critics call ἦθος,
the quiet play of character. First comes an Honest
Man, long since reduced to penury, but now
prosperous, who comes to dedicate the old threadbare cloak he has worn for thirteen years, and
some indescribable shoes. He is followed by a
'sŷcophantês', ruined and in the worst of tempers.
Here for a moment the old lion wakes, and we have
for a hundred lines a thoroughly scathing treatment of the Informer. The man explains that he
is a public benefactor. The laws are always being
broken. No one but he attends to the offences,
yet he is always ready to do his duty. It is for
ὁ βουλόμενος ('Any one who will') to give information, and he is ὁ βουλόμενος ('Some one who will').
He is stripped and beaten off in the old way, with
the Honest Man's ragged cloak about his naked-
ness and the Honest Man's shoes fastened as a
crown about his head.

Next comes a rather unpleasing character, who
seems almost repeated from the final scene of the
Ecclesiazûsae, an Old Woman, who has hitherto
had a young man acting as her lover because of her
riches. The scene is not coarse, like that in the
Ecclesiazûsae, but it does strike a modern English
reader as ungentlemanly: the chaff of the Old
Woman is not funny enough to redeem it from
cruelty, though it is something of a satisfaction to
find in the end that she is given the best of it, and

the mercenary young man is compelled to con-
tinue his servitude. The Old Woman accompanies
him into the house.

The stage is empty when a miserable figure
timidly knocks on the door—and is so frightened
that he immediately denies that he has done so.
He is Hermes, the God of Craft, the messenger of
Zeus, now reduced to a state of extreme neediness.
Nevertheless, he begins, as in duty bound, with
threats. 'Zeus is wroth. The sacrifices have
stopped. You have all committed a great sin, and
must be destroyed.' 'All of you come out in order
of rank,' he says to Carion, 'Your master, his wife,
his children, the servants, the dog, yourself, and
the pig,' a nice hierarchy. But his bluff is soon
called, and he is only too willing to desert the
impoverished service of Zeus and accept that of
Chremylus and Wealth. Unfortunately they have
no work for him; neither as Turner (Strophaios),
nor Twister (Dolios), nor Merchant (Empolaios),
nor Guide (Hêgemonios). However, he is also
God of Games (Enagônios). There may be something for him to do in that capacity. How useful
it is to have many different trades!

The last visitor is the Priest of Zeus Sôtêr himself, come to take refuge with Wealth and Chremylus since no one now frequents the temples at all.
Plutus just looks at people; if they are good he
stays with them, if they are bad he leaves them—
so why should they care about sacrificing to the

Olympians? The conscientious Priest has some qualms about his desertion, but is comforted as well as startled by the information that his God has been before him. Zeus Sôtêr himself has deserted his temple and is already inside the house! The various characters come forth, and the play ends in a great procession, in which the Old Woman and her attendant suitor take their part.

A fairly amusing play produced under poverty-stricken conditions. We have noticed already that wealth for the Athenian citizen at this time seems to have meant the certainty of having enough food to eat. The old playwright had finished his public work, ending so to speak in a *diminuendo*, in a play with less noise in it, less passion, and less vitality. But he was not at the end of his own intellectual resources. He wrote two comedies after this time, and gave them to some one else to produce, just as he had given his earliest efforts to Philônides and Callistratus. The two latest plays he gave to his son, Arârôs, who intended to be a playwright and was in this way started on his career. Arârôs afterwards seems to have been a fairly successful writer.

One of the plays was called *Aiolosikôn*; a compound name, like 'Dionysalexandros' or 'Heracleioxanthias.' Sikôn was a proverbial cook: the name seems to be a short slave-name for Σικελός. Apparently either Aeolus in the play was acting as a cook, or, conceivably, a cook behaving like Aeolus.

The other was named *Kôkalus*, after a mythical
king of Camîcus in Sicily who had been the hero of
Sophocles' tragedy, *The Camicians*. Thus both the
plays were of a type which had indeed occurred in
the Old Comedy—witness the *Odyssês* of Cratinus
and at least three plays of Plato Comicus—but became exceedingly common at the beginning of
the fourth century; a burlesque or parody of some
tragic theme. The *Aiolosikôn* seems to have parodied Euripides' tragedy, *Aeolus*, which in turn
was based on the Homeric story of Aeolus, king
of the winds, with his six sons married to his six
daughters, for ever feasting in a great hall on their
floating island. Homer implies that they had only
one Hall: so in Aristophanes they have only one
bedroom and one bath. The burlesque of heroic
story, the great preoccupation with cookery and
feasting, and doubtless the absence of Chorus made
the ancient critics treat this play as starting the
type of the 'Middle Comedy'.[1] The Kôkalus
legend told how Minos of Crete, when pursuing
Daedalus, eventually overtook him at the court
of Kôkalus. Kôkalus, unable to resist Minos' over-
powering forces yet unwilling to give up his guest,
entertained Minos and killed him in his bath. But
we are told in the ancient *Life* of Aristophanes that
the *Kôkalus* started the type of the New Comedy,
since it 'introduced a seduction and a recognition
and all the other features which Menander delighted

[1] Platonius, περὶ Διαφορᾶς κωμῳδιῶν.

in'. One may conjecture that there was a love-story and an intrigue between Daedalus and one of the daughters of the king; if there was a 'recognition' in the style of Menander, it must almost certainly have been the recognition of an exposed or kidnapped baby; and it would be easy enough, from such a treatment of the story, to lead to a more complicated plot in which Kôkalus is persuaded by his daughter not to betray her lover but instead to kill his enemy.

The statement in the *Life* may well be exaggerated; one cannot build upon it with certainty. Yet, such as it is, it holds the field, and if we accept it we obtain a striking picture of the life-work of this wonderful man. In his youth he saw undreamed-of possibilities in the rude phallic dance and song which was the Kômos of Dionysus. At first he hardly cared to appear on the stage himself, but he wrote Comedies, gradually purifying and intellectualizing the strange performance without ever losing its boisterous fun or reducing its intense vitality; he raised its invective from mere orgies of comic abuse to expressions of high political indignation and even idealism; he fought against overwhelming odds for the cause of justice, or generosity, towards the Athenian allies, for what he considered the old spirit of Aristîdes, and most of all for peace. He was defeated in public affairs; so he turned more exclusively towards art and poetry and perfected his instrument—an instrument peculiar to one place and time and never rediscovered in human history. He saw this instrument decay and break in his hands, made impossible partly by lack of public funds, partly by the ever-increasing reign of fear in politics, partly by that rise in the level of refinement in which he himself had been the prime mover. He became tired and made compromises, but on the whole still wrote plays which would have been hailed as works of genius if he had not done so much better before. He retired at last from the stage, with a last play, quiet, good-natured, and showing no bitterness at a world that imagined it had outgrown him. And then, in his retirement, he wrote—and handed over to his son for production—a play of a new type altogether, a story of individual life, with character and intrigue and emotion, a beginning, it would seem, of that art-form with which Menander fifty or sixty years afterwards was to conquer the theatrical world and point the way for all successive writers of modern comedy.

It is certainly significant that the *Plutus*, which seems to us moderns about the weakest of Aristophanes' plays, should on the whole have been the most popular in later antiquity. It is not merely that the Byzantine doctors found it the most suitable for school use. Soon after the author's death there was a rapid change of taste. An age which was really repelled and bewildered by the Old Comedy found the *Plutus* less offensive than any of Aristophanes' earlier plays, less unintelligible, and, in fact, less unlike Menander.

For by the beginning of the third century B.C. Menander had become not only the most successful dramatist but the recognized model of style. Public affairs were then no longer a live issue for those outside the court and the army, so the key to most of Aristophanes' emotion was lost. Lyrical poetry had become little more than a *tour de force* for the learned, so that much of his beauty was lost. His extravagance no longer charmed, and the simplicity of his fun, with its puns and horseplay and old-fashioned jokes, had become tedious to a less high-spirited and more sophisticated society. The striking phrase 'a mirror of human life', which Aristotle had selected as an example of frigidity and affectation when it was first used,[1] survived his censure and became the recognized statement of an ideal. Such a 'mirror' was found and admired in the *Odyssey*, in various mimes, above all in Menander; an extant verse of the Alexandrian scholar, Aristophanes of Byzantium, expressed this admiration:

> O Menander, and O Life,
> Which of you is the copy of the other?[2]

We attempt in the next chapter to give some

---

[1] By Alcidamas, of the *Odyssey*: Ar. *Rhetoric.* Γ. 3, 4.

[2] 	῏Ω Μένανδρε καὶ βίε,
    πότερος ἄρ' ὑμῶν πότερον ἀπεμιμήσατο;

account of this second great luminary of the Greek comic stage, of whose work we possess more than a thousand fragments but no single complete play. The contrast between him and Aristophanes is startling, and it is interesting to collect from the scanty remains of Greek criticism some signs of the rapid change of taste which led from the one to the other.

From the fourth century to Alexandrian times literary taste lay under the spell of Aristotle and his School, and Aristotle, great critic as he was, was not the man to delight in the Old Comedy. He was the first to put aside the crude popular tests of utility and edification and to judge poetry by aesthetic standards. He was reasonable, acute, witty, and amazingly well informed and well read. He was highly civilized and urbane, and set store on various qualities which were not exactly the strong suit of Aristophanes. He quite sees that there is a place in life for fun and comedy, but explains in the *Ethics* that, being parts of life, they must come under the normal rules of life.

First, he asks, are there any principles at all in these light subjects? 'Yes,' he decides (*Eth. Nic.* 1127 b 33):

Since life includes rest, and rest involves leisure and amusement (παιδία), there seems here also to be a kind of social intercourse that is ἐμμελής (harmonious?). There is such a thing as saying—and listening to—the sort of thing one should and in the way one should.

Evidently here too there can be a 'Too-much' and a 'Too-little'. Those who pursue the Laughable too much are considered buffoons and vulgar (φορτικοί), striving after humour at all costs, and caring more about raising a laugh than about saying what is seemly and not hurting the feelings of the object of the joke. . . . To the middle state also belongs ἐπιδεξιότης (Tact?). It is a mark of tact to say and listen to the sort of things that are fitting to a good and well-bred man (ἐπιεικεῖ καὶ ἐλευθερίωι). For there are some things which it befits such a man to say—and hear—by way of amusement; and the amusement of the well-bred man differs from that of the vulgar, and that of the educated from that of the uneducated. One can see this from the comedies of the old and the new style. To the old comedy foul language was funny, while the new finds suggestion more so, which makes a great difference in decency.

The word translated 'suggestion' (ὑπόνοια), I should explain, has not the connotation of impropriety attached to the English 'suggestive'.

Now should we define the good joke as that which is not unbefitting to a gentleman (ἐλευθερίωι), or as that which does not give pain to the person addressed, but rather pleasure? Or is that sort of definition also indefinite, since different people find different things pleasant or unpleasant?[1]

[1] Compare also his strong feeling that the infliction of pain is not funny: ψόγος (blame or satire) is quite different from τὸ γελοῖον (the laughable) (*Poet.* 1448 b 24 ff.). Comedy represents the lower type of man. It arises in democracies, in connexion with democratic freedom of speech. At first we have ψόγοι (satires) as opposed to songs and praises: then an advance from satire to the laughable (τὸ γελοῖον). The ridiculous implies a flaw and ugliness not painful and not destructive, e.g. the comic mask, ugly and distorted with no suggestion of pain.

Later we have the very emphatic statement: 'Ridicule is a kind of abusive language. The law forbids certain forms of abusive language: it ought perhaps to forbid certain forms of jesting.' 'Foul language above all (εἴπερ τι ἄλλο) ought to be banished by law from the state.' (Cf. *Pol.* 1336 b 3.)

More direct and more impassioned is the criticism of Aristophanes in the fragment of a Comparison between Aristophanes and Menander which is found among Plutarch's *Moralia*. Whether by Plutarch or not, one must recognize that the passage evidently comes from a Dialogue and that all this vehement condemnation must have had an equally emphatic answer from some admirer of Aristophanes, an answer, however, which is most unfortunately lost. Plutarch, *Moralia*, p. 853 (vol. v, p. 203 Bernardakis):

There is a vulgar, theatrical and common quality in Aristophanes' language, and not at all in Menander's. The man in the street (ἰδιώτης) is caught by his writing, but the man of culture offended. I mean especially the antitheses and rhymes and similarities of sound, e.g. ταμίαι, Λαμίαι; καικίας, συκοφαντίας; γελῶτα, Γέλαν. Then in his choice of words we have the tragic and the comic, the grand and common, obscurity and ordinariness, pomp and elevation mixed with babbling and nonsense to make one sick. Yet, with all those differences and incongruities, his diction does not give the appropriate and natural language to each character— dignity to the king, cleverness to the rhetor, simplicity to the woman, ordinary words to the ordinary citizen and vulgarity to the vulgar; but tosses out by lot, as it were, the first words that come to any speaker, so that you cannot tell if he is a son, a father, a rustic, a god, an old woman or a hero.

Now Menander's language (φράσις) is so tempered, so polished and so pervaded by one atmosphere, that while passing through many passions and feelings and fitted to all kinds of characters, it yet seems one and preserves its character. . . .

[Some writers appeal to the few, some to the many] . . . But Aristophanes is neither pleasing to the many nor tolerable to the thinking few. His poetry is like an old harlot who has passed her prime and imitates a very respectable married woman; the many cannot endure her airs, and the cultured (σεμνοί) are disgusted by her immorality and spitefulness. While Menander. . . . [Here follows an account of his popularity.]

Menander's comedies are full of salt, abundant and without bitterness, as if they were born from that sea from which Aphrodite sprang. But the salt of Aristophanes is bitter and harsh, with an astringency that bites and wounds. And I cannot see wherein that Δεξιότης (cleverness?) that he boasts of lies, in the words or the characters. Even what he does represent he distorts for the worse. His rascals are not like fellow-creatures, but malignant beings;[1] his rustics not simple but idiotic; his laughter not playful but full of scorn, his treatment of love not gay but lascivious. The man seems never to have written for decent readers.

Let us hope that there was a good fighting answer from the admirer of Aristophanes. Its loss is the more regrettable because we really have

---

[1] Or 'his cleverness is not sociable but malicious'?

almost no appreciative criticism of Aristophanes in ancient literature. The nearest approach, perhaps, is a short passage in Quintilian (x. i. 65):

> The Old Comedy is almost alone in preserving the true charm (*sinceram gratiam*) of Attic speech; at the same time it has the most expressive freedom of speech (*facundissimae libertatis*), especially in denouncing vice, though it is full of strength all through. It is grand, elegant, and charming (*grandis, elegans, venusta*), and— Homer always excepted, like Achilles—I doubt if any other literature is more akin to oratory or more suitable for making orators.

This shows appreciation. The language of Horace, I think, hardly does so. He seems to have fallen back on a very conventional position, that these ancient poets are very classical and celebrated, and no doubt did good service in rebuking vice, but were regrettably violent in their language and had to be stopped (*Sat.* i. 4. 1).

> Eupolis atque Cratinus Aristophanesque poetae
> Atque alii quorum Comoedia prisca virorum est
> Si quis erat dignus describi, quod malus aut fur,
> Quod moechus foret aut sicarius aut alioqui
> Famosus, multa cum libertate notabant.

Cf. *Ars Poetica* 281:

> Successit vetus his Comoedia, non sine multa
> Laude; sed in vitium libertas excidit et vim
> Dignam lege regi. Lex est accepta, Chorusque
> Turpiter obticuit, sublato iure nocendi.

Free speech about dignitaries was not considered good taste at the Courts of Ptolemy or Augustus.

The real defence of Aristophanes seems to have
been inarticulate but none the less effective. The
romantic movement in Alexandria, loving what
was antique and strange and imaginative, revived
the interest in the Old Comedy. The great Erato-
sthenes, the poet and critic who also measured
the earth and invented longitude, seems to have
been the leader of the movement. He wrote Περὶ
'Αρχαίας Κωμῳδίας; and we have in the scholia not
only a long list of distinguished scholars who discussed particular passages—Didymus, Lycophron,
Euphronius, Dionysiades, and even the *rex criti-
corum*, Aristarchus—but a greater mass of erudition
and research than exists for any other author except Homer and possibly Pindar. Critics might
prove that the Old Comedy was just a mass of
faults; undue abuse of individuals, language unfit
for a gentleman, childish puns, and plays on words.
They might prove that it was not like life, that it
showed no subtlety in character-drawing, no power
whatever of construction or plot. Nevertheless
there were evidently plenty of students and literary
men, at any rate, who would answer Plutarch's
comparison with the words

τὸν μὲν ἡγοῦμαι σοφόν, τῷ δ᾽ ἥδομαι.

Menander was no doubt a most accomplished
writer, but they loved Aristophanes—and there
was an end to it.

It is difficult, even with our richer and subtler
vocabulary of criticism, to make an adequate

answer to Plutarch's imaginary critic. One can
see that he is concerned merely with style. He
takes no account of the historical conditions under
which Aristophanes did his work, and makes no
attempt to understand the purpose or spirit of his
writings. Then, even in the question of style, his
interests are those of the ordinary school of 'rhêto-
rikê'. He looks out for clarity, appropriateness,
elegance, simplicity, absence of extravagance or
affectation; he does not think about those qualities
which go beyond the requirements of correct
academic prose, such as sublimity, creative power,
unexpectedness, wild humour or poetic imagination. But above all, one can see that, from beginning to end, he is taking the New Comedy as his
standard and judging Aristophanes thereby, demanding of him qualities which he never aimed
at and paying no attention to those which he really
has. He reminds one of the judgements passed by
eighteenth-century critics on Shakespeare, or of
Neo-Georgians who shudder at Dickens because
he has not the restraint of Mr. Galsworthy.

It would be too easy a way out of the difficulty
to say that the quality which they ignore is simply
genius, that unanalysable power which Plato and
Aristotle call μανικόν, or 'akin to madness', and
which the latter prudently leaves out of account
in the *Poetics*. But certainly there is in Aristophanes an exuberance of life, like that which
enables Dickens and Shakespeare to create by the

dozen characters who stand out as immortal in
English literature. Such vitality may, no doubt,
often go with carelessness in writing or construction, violence, lack of proportion, offences against
strict canons of taste, but on the other hand it
does create standards of its own and can achieve a
positive beauty of expression which is denied to
most of the less faulty and less vital artists. It is
tediousness that kills. I doubt whether any writer
has lasted very long whose style had not, page
by page, some real charm or beauty. Style and
creative power: those are perhaps the two greatest
literary qualities. Aristophanes has both, and adds
to them a third, a fundamentally sound and cour-
ageous 'criticism of life'. That is, I think, the
reason of his extraordinary freshness.

Humour is a wine that soon loses its savour.
Think how soon even old *Punches* begin to date,
how stale often are the facetiae of Molière and of
Shakespeare, how difficult to read are Erasmus and
Rabelais, and how intolerable the Comedy of the
Middle Ages! The style seems lumbering. The
jokes have begun to bore us before the point
comes. The humour seems rough, dull, unpercep-
tive, obvious, often cruel; the whole outlook on life
dead and conventional. And then turn to Aristophanes. His date is immensely remote from ours;
his art-form is one utterly strange to us, and one
which we should never dream of reviving. His
frequent indecency is such as we could not tolerate

in our own language. Yet for some strange reason
the bloom is still on him. His jokes are our jokes.
His interests are really interesting. His style is un-
forced and vivid in its natural charm—*grandis et
venusta et elegans*, as Quintilian said. One feels,
also, beyond the mere verbal style, the intellectual
power of the man, the idealism, the courage, the
unexpectedness, the lyric beauty . . . and reading
him one laughs aloud.

CHAPTER X

MENANDER, AND THE TRANSFORMATION OF COMEDY

MENANDER, son of Diopeithes, the chief poet of the Athenian New Comedy, is a figure difficult to estimate. He was born in the year 342 B.C., only some forty years after the death of Aristophanes, but into an Athens which was greatly changed. He must have heard Aristotle; he was on friendly terms with Epicurus. He lived practically all his life under the rule of the Macedonians, and died in 290 when the first Ptolemy was already king in Egypt and the first Seleucus in Syria. His fame was immense. He is constantly quoted by later authors, including of course St. Paul: 'Evil communications corrupt good manners.'[1] But until lately he was known only through these quotations and through the Latin imitations of his work by Plautus and Terence; even now, after the great discoveries of papyri, though we have seven hundred lines of one play and considerable remains of several more, we have no single comedy complete.

But the mystery does not come merely from lack of information. The things that we do know about Menander are hard to combine. The

---

[1] 1 Cor. xv. 33, from the Θαΐς, 218. I quote the fragments from Kock's *Comicorum Atticorum Fragmenta*, vol. iii (1888).

quotations have a quality of their own. They not only show simplicity and distinction of language; they also seem to be the expression of a refined, thoughtful, and very sympathetic mind, touched with melancholy but remarkably free from passion or sensuality. Let us consider a few:

Whom the gods love die young. (125)

I am man, and nothing that belongs to man
Is alien from me.[1]

How sweet life is, can we but choose with whom
To live! 'Tis no life, living for oneself.

(506, 507; cf. 531.)

All sufferers have one refuge, a good friend,
To whom they can lay bare their griefs and know
He will not smile. (543)

Poor mortal, never pray to have no griefs,
Pray to have fortitude. (549)

An attitude towards life comes out in the lines:

We live not as we will, but as we can. (50; cf. 590, 604.)

Nay, Gorgias, I call him the bravest man,
Who knows to suffer the most injuries
With patience. All this swiftness of resentment
Is proof of a little mind. (95)

Fight not with God, nor to the storm without
Add your own storms. (187)

What stings you is the lightest of all ills,
Mere poverty . . . a thing one friend can cure. (282)

(Cf. 301 on what money can do and can not do.)

[1] This famous line is not extant in the Greek: the Latin is in Terence, *Heaut.* I. i. 25 (*Homo sum, humani nil a me alienum puto*).

This spirit of resignation leads to a sort of theoretic anarchism or antinomianism:

> The man who does no evil needs no law. (845)

It is character that shapes a man's life. This is expounded at length in the chief extant play, *The Arbitration* (ll. 659-72); and briefly in fr. 594.

> Fortune is no real thing.
> But men who cannot bear what comes to them
> In Nature's way, give their own characters
> The name of Fortune.

Lastly, to keep the true savour of Menander in one's mind, there is the great passage in fr. 481:

> I count it happiness,
> Ere we go quickly thither whence we came,
> To gaze ungrieving on these majesties,
> The world-wide sun, the stars, water and clouds,
> And fire. Live, Parmeno, a hundred years
> Or a few months, these you will always see,
> And never, never, any greater things.
>
> Think of this lifetime as a festival
> Or visit to a strange city, full of noise,
> Buying and selling, thieving, dicing-stalls
> And joy-parks. If you leave it early, friend,
> Why, think you have gone to find a better inn;
> You have paid your fare and leave no enemies.

Or again:

> My son, you do not see,
> How everything that dies, dies by its own
> Corruption: all that injures is within.
> Rust is the bane of iron, moths of wool,

And worms of wood; in you there is a bane
Most deadly, which has made you sick to death
And makes and shall make—envy. (540.)

How comes it that the man who writes these
gentle refined thoughts, full of self-restraint and
philosophy, is the chief author of the Athenian
New Comedy, known to us mainly by the grotesque comic masks found on vases and frescoes,
and by the rather coarse-grained and dissolute
imitations of Plautus and Terence: plays in which
the heroines are generally either prostitutes or girls
who have illegitimate children, and the heroes
worthless young rakes, while the most amusing
character is often a rascally slave engaged in
swindling the hero's father or uncle out of large
sums of money to pay to brothel-keepers, or else
in burgling the brothels themselves; in which
foundlings and exposed children are recovered
and recognized with bewildering monotony, and
the list of stock characters so limited and mechan-
ical, that an ancient writer on the Theatre[1] can
give you a list of all the masks that a company
needs to stock in order to produce any play? It
all seems at first sight so coarse, so stupid and
lacking in invention, so miserably shallow in its
view of life.

The ordinary explanation is that Menander was
just an elegant but dissipated person with a fine
style but no ideals, writing for a corrupt society

[1] Pollux. *Onom.* iv. 143 sqq.

which had lost all its sense of freedom, religion, and public duty. Let us quote, as typical of the best current criticism, Professor Wilhelm Schmid:[1]

While recognizing fully the aesthetic and technical merits of these plays, we must not pass over their ethical flatness, invertebracy, and lack of temperament. All forms of strength are transformed into elegance and smoothness for the amusement of a generation which can stand nothing rude or harsh, and is equally averse to all impetus, idealism, or artistic daring. . . . All is indulgence and hushing up, a frivolous trifling with all moral conceptions, with truth and honour; . . . a moral twilight, in which all sound standards of value become invisible.

Other critics have compared the New Comedy to the Comedy of the English Restoration, and Menander to Congreve or Wycherley, with their wit, their grossness, their narrow range, and their 'hearts like the nether millstone'. But I venture to think that all this criticism, like much else that is written about the Hellenistic period, errs through neglecting an important clue.

One cannot understand the thought of this period, particularly that of the Stoic or the Epicurean school, except as a response of the human soul to an almost blinding catastrophe of defeat and disenchantment. All that a fifth-century Athenian had believed in had failed and been found wanting. The gods could neither save their worshippers nor bear the criticism of their rejectors. As for

[1] Christ, *Griech. Lit.*[6] ii. 1, p. 36.

Athens, her continued attempt to be a Tyrant City was ridiculous: she was barely strong enough to 'stand alone in the strenuous conditions of modern life'. She could no longer be regarded as a unique object of almost religious devotion. She was not sufficiently important, in a world where there were millions of human beings, nor, if it comes to that, sufficiently superior in 'wisdom and justice' to the average run of unsatisfactory mankind. Nay, wisdom and justice themselves did not seem to matter as much as the philosophers had pretended. Unlettered scoundrels with large mercenary armies behind them seemed mostly to be inheriting the earth, at least until their throats were cut by others of the same kind.[1]

The reaction of Hellenistic Athens to this moral and civil chaos, produced by the long scrambles for empire among the generals who divided Alexander's inheritance, seems almost always to start with some admission of the vanity of human wishes and the deceitfulness of this world. The general wreck was admitted, but each school sought to save something out of the wreck on which to support the human soul. 'All is vanity except Virtue;' said the Cynic and the Stoic, 'Man can at least do his duty until death.' 'All except pleasure;' said the Epicurean, 'that man should be happy at least is indisputably good.' 'All except success;' said the military adventurers, 'let fools talk about justice

[1] Compare for this atmosphere the fragments of Theopompus.

or religion; the one solid good is to have power and money.' It was in much the same spirit that Demosthenes, after the crash of all his efforts, had discovered that he could at least still die for Athens, and Plato that amid a raving world he could at least try to keep his eyes on eternal truth.

The response of Menander is more complicated, and consequently less impassioned. He is not a professional philosopher; he is a writer of Comedy, an Athenian gentleman, a product of high civilization and culture, whose natural world has been broken up and is under the heel of soldiers and money-lenders. What remains to him out of the wreck is a sense of keen interest in the spectacle of life, and an infinite belief in patience, affection, and sympathy. He is always urging that men are not so bad as they would seem from their actions. 'They do not what they will, but what they can.' Their antics make him smile, but seldom alienate him, except when some one makes bad things worse by harshness to others, or envy or pride.

True, there is very little religion in his plays; and there seems to have been a good deal of satire against superstition. There is little or no Athenian patriotism: he was fellow-citizen to all humanity. His love of Athens showed itself in practice by his steadily refusing all the invitations to leave it that came to him from Ptolemy and perhaps from other kings. His moral judgements possibly err on the side of indulgence, but it is not the indulgence of

indifference or of cynicism. They have the same
kind of refinement and sensitiveness that has made
famous his literary style. At least so it seems to
me. Yet I know that the orthodox critics will
ask how I can say such a thing, when his plays
are all about dissipated young men and illegitimate children, cheating slaves, brothel-keepers, and
prostitutes.

I will explain why I venture to say it. In the
first place all these crude terms are inexact. And to
understand Menander one has first of all to realize
the strange conditions of the time and the hardness
with which they bore upon women.[1]

In the old City-State there were theoretically
only two kinds of women: the citizeness who could
be lawfully married to a citizen, and the slave or
foreign woman who could not. The slave might
be owned by the citizen with whom she lived, or
she might belong to a speculator, a *leno*, who kept
her for sale or hire. In practice there were also
resident foreigners with their perfectly respectable
wives; there were also women of good birth and
character, but foreign nationality, who were not
legally able to marry a citizen, but could contract
a free union with him.

In the age of Alexander and his successors this
state of affairs, already difficult, was further com-

---

[1] The biography of Menander in Suidas describes him as 'madly
devoted to women'; he seems at any rate, as a sort of intellectual champion of women, to have taken on the heritage of Euripides.

plicated by constant wars, sieges, and transfers of
population. When a town was taken, there was
not, indeed, a massacre of the men and a wholesale
violation of the women, such as was common in the
Middle Ages or the Thirty Years' War; but there
was often a great *andrapodismos*, or sale of slaves.
The slave-dealers and *lenones* were waiting behind
the lines, and bought human flesh cheap.[1] It was
in this period that the great slave markets of Delos
and Rhodes came into existence, and after every
campaign there were hundreds of women and
children sold hither and thither about the Greek
world, or held by the *lenones* for the purpose of
their infamous traffic. It is women of this sort,
the victims of war, mostly friendless and the sport
of circumstance, whom Menander so often chooses
for his heroines. The titles of many plays—*The
Woman of Andros, of Olynthus, of Perinthus, of
Samos*—tell the story plainly enough; and the harp-
player, Habrotonon, in *The Arbitration*, with her
generous recklessness and her longing for freedom,
probably had the same history behind her. In
many plays the woman is the property of a soldier:
he bought her cheap on the spot, no doubt, or
perhaps got her as a prize. The facts are brutal,
but the human beings are much the reverse. In
one play (*Hated*) the Soldier has fallen in love

---

[1] In Xenophon's Life of Agesilaus (i. 21) it is mentioned how the
slave-traders hung about besieged cities, and how sometimes, when
things grew dangerous, they had to fly, leaving their wares behind.

with his captive, but will not touch her or trouble her because the frightened girl has told him that she hates him. He walks out alone at night and thinks of suicide. In others some generous or amorous youth tries desperately to collect the necessary sum to buy the girl's freedom from the *leno* who owns her, or to outbid or forestall the soldier who has arranged to buy her. In others, despairing of lawful purchase, he gets together a band of friends who storm the *leno's* house and carry the girl off by force. It is all for her good, and every *leno* deserves worse than the worst he gets. No doubt sometimes these women showed one sort of character, sometimes another; and sometimes they just lapsed into the ways of vice serenely, with a professional eye to the main chance: the two *Bacchides* of Plautus are an instance, and they are taken from Menander. But it is quite misleading to talk without further explanation of 'prostitutes' and 'brothels'. One might better compare these people with the great populations of refugees scattered about the world of recent years, the Russian 'whites' in Constantinople, the exiles from the Baltic Republics, or the 'stateless persons' of eastern Europe. There would probably be the same variety of fortune and character, though the absence of professional slave-traders has doubtless left our present refugees in a condition of greater hope, if perhaps of less security.

Another of Menander's favourite characters is

the exposed child, who is eventually discovered and recognized by its repentant parents. It was an old mythical motive: the Oedipus story made use of it; Euripides' *Ion*, *Antiopê*, *Augê*, *Melanippê*, *Alopê* and other tragedies, were based upon it. It survived to shape the story of Romulus and Remus, and the many foundling-heroes of medieval romance. I have little doubt, though of course the point cannot be proved, that this baby is merely a humanized form of the divine Year-Baby which is the regular hero of the traditional 'Mummers' Play' and of many Greek rituals. Now it is likely enough that in this matter Menander was led away by the attractions of a romantic motive which was already canonized in ancient tradition, and which provided plenty of dramatic thrill with a minimum of trouble. But of course it is to be remembered also that the exposure of children was all through antiquity permitted by law, if generally condemned by public opinion. And if permitted by law, it was certain in a time of great changes of fortune to be practised. The commonest reason for exposing a child then, as now, was the desire to conceal an illegitimate birth. But there were others. Pataecus, in the *Perikeiromenê* ('*He clips her Hair*'), finds seventeen or eighteen years later the children whom he had exposed in their infancy. They cannot believe that he, who has always seemed so kind, would have done such a thing. But he explains that his wife had died in giving birth to

them, and the day before her death he had learned
that the ship which contained his whole fortune
had been wrecked. He could not rear the children,
so he put rich gifts with them and left them beside
a shrine.

These foundlings—who in imitation of their
mythical or semi-divine prototypes[1] are apt to be
twins—cause the humane playwright a good deal
of trouble. In heroic legend the father is normally
a god, and of course nobody as a rule ventures to
characterize the action of the god as it deserves.
Even the angry father who is about to kill the
princess for her breach of chastity is softened when
he learns the high rank of her accomplice. But
Menander, in taking over the legendary motive
into common contemporary life, has to give the
bastard a human father, and yet not make the
father a scoundrel. Sometimes he evades the difficulty by putting the false step into the distant past,
and letting the guilty old gentleman drop a quiet
tear over the errors of his youth. But his commonest device is a nocturnal religious festival. We
have enough evidence about May-day festivals in
Europe as late as the seventeenth century to show
us that these ancient celebrations of the fertility
of the spring retained through thousands of years,
in the teeth of all law and decorum, strong traces
of that communal marriage-feast in which they

---

[1] e.g. Romulus and Remus, Amphion and Zethus, Boeotus and
Aeolus.

originated. And it is likely enough that in the wild
emotion of the midnight dances in wood and on
mountain many an excited girl met her ravisher.
In the only scene extant which treats fully of such
an incident, what strikes one most is the bitter
repentance of the youth. In *The Arbitration*
(*Epitrepontes*) it so happens that Charisius learns
that a few months after marriage his wife Pamphilê
has secretly given birth to a child. He is reluctant
to publish his dishonour, and he still loves his wife.
So he treats her with marked neglect and spends
most of his time away, pretending to enjoy himself, but really eating his heart out. Then he discovers that last year, at the midnight festival of the
Tauropolia, Pamphilê, who had got separated from
her companions, was ravished in the dark by an
unknown man; and he knows, by his memory of
that night, that he must have been the man! A
Congreve hero would have concealed the fact and
doubtless handsomely forgiven the lady; but
Menander's young scapegrace is wild with self-
reproach. He does not merely recognize that he
is in the same boat with Pamphilê; he sees that he
is guilty and she is innocent, and furthermore that
he has behaved like a bully and a prig and a hypo-
crite, while she has steadily defended him against
her indignant father.

Let us take one more case to illustrate both the
brutality of the times and the delicacy of feeling
with which the cultivated Athenian confronted it.

When Pataecus, as mentioned above, exposed his
two children, they were picked up together with
their tokens, or means of recognition, by an old
woman. She passed the boy, Moschio, on to a rich
woman, Myrrhinê, who was pining for a child,
and who brought the foundling up as her own son.
As for the girl, Glycera, the old woman kept her,
and eventually, as she felt death approaching, revealed to her the facts of her birth, told her that
Moschio was her brother, and advised her, if ever
she wanted help, to go to the Rich Lady, Myrrhinê,
who knew all. Then, since the girl needed a protector, and a respectable soldier was in love with
her, the old woman gave her to the soldier. She
was not his wife: probably a legal marriage was
not possible. She was certainly not a slave. She
was free, as we find stated in the play, either to live
with him or to leave him.

All goes well till one evening Glycera, standing
at her door, sees her brother Moschio looking at
her with interest. She guesses—wrongly—that he
has been told that she is his sister, and this guess is
confirmed when he runs up and kisses her. She
returns the kiss. Her soldier sees her; Moschio,
who is a young fop and had merely kissed her
because she looked pretty and smiled, runs away.
The soldier is transported with rage. Had he been
an Englishman, at most periods of history he would
have beaten her. Had he been an Italian, he might
have murdered her. Being an Athenian, he cuts

her hair off. This outrage gives the play its name
(*Perikeiromenê*, '*He clips her Hair*'), and from our
present point of view it is interesting to see how it
is regarded by the people concerned. The soldier
goes away furious with himself and everybody
else; he drinks in order to forget his grief, and is
divided between a wish to humble himself and
make it up and a wish to kill Moschio. Glycera
herself considers the insult unpardonable, leaves
the soldier's house, and takes refuge with the
Rich Lady, as her old guardian had told her to
do. When the soldier tells the story, as he understands it, to Pataecus, that quiet man of the world
tells him that he has behaved disgracefully: Glycera
is not his slave. She has a perfect right to leave
him if she likes, and also a right to take up with
Moschio; and that in any case no self-respecting
woman will live with a person who may at any
moment cut her hair off.

PATAECUS. Of course, if she had been your wife . . .
SOLDIER. What a thing to say! If!
PAT. Well, there is a difference.
SOL. I regard Glycera as my wife.
PAT. Who gave her in marriage to you?
SOL. She herself.

'Very good,' says Pataecus. 'No doubt she
liked you then, and now she has left you because
you have not treated her properly. . . .'
'Not treated her properly!' cries the poor
soldier, 'That hurts me . . .', and he goes on later

to explain how entirely well and respectfully he has treated her, except for this one act of madness. 'Just let me show you her wardrobe,' he adds; and by that ingenious device Pataecus is made, later on, to see the signet ring and the necklace that he had left with his exposed child.

Meantime, since the soldier is genuinely penitent, Pataecus will try to persuade Glycera to return. When he does so, Glycera is outraged to find that he also has misinterpreted the kiss she gave to Moschio, and even imagined that it was in pursuit of Moschio that she fled to his supposed mother's house. 'You knew me, and you thought me capable of that!'

The point which I wish to make clear is this. Menander is not merely the ingenious favourite of a corrupt and easy-going society. Athenian society in his day, I would suggest, had as a whole assimilated the liberal sensitiveness that was confined to a few exceptional personalities in the previous century; the average cultivated Athenian now felt instinctively much as Plato or Euripides felt. But the ordered world of the fifth century, precarious even then, had now crumbled away. The ordinary Athenian gentleman, who had formerly lived a strenuous life in patriotic military service, in domestic or imperial politics, in the duties of his hereditary priesthoods, in the management of his estates, now found his occupation gone. Politics consisted in obeying the will of a foreign military

governor; military service meant enlistment as a
mercenary under some foreign adventurer; local
priesthoods were little more than antiquarian
hobbies, things of no reality and no importance;
and the Athenian landed proprietor was, by the
new standards, only a poor farmer. All public
activity was dangerous. 'Keep quiet and study;
keep quiet and practise virtue; keep quiet and
enjoy yourself: but at all events keep quiet. And
remember that even then you are not safe.' When
Menander was a boy of seven, Thebes, one of the
greatest of Greek cities, was razed to the ground
by the Macedonians and the whole population sold
into slavery. The horror of the deed rang through
Greece. When the poet was about twenty, Antipater put a garrison into Athens, and deported all
citizens who possessed less than 2,000 drachmae,
which meant exile for more than half the citizen
body. Next year, Antipater being dead, one of
his rivals changed the constitution again; the exiles
swarmed back, only to be crushed and driven out
once more by Antipater's son, Cassander. Samos
was depopulated twice. It became, for some two
generations at least, a common incident of war that
cities should be sacked and populations sold into
slavery; and this is probably the reason for the
immense increase in the proportion of slaves[1] to

[1] Athen. vi, p. 272 c: in 317 B.C., under Demetrius of Phalêrum
21,000 citizens in Athens, 10,000 metoikoi, 400,000 slaves. Cf. the
speeches in Polybius xvii. 2, 3 about the conduct of Philip V, who was
carrying on the habits of the Diadochi. Cf. also Livy 38. 43; 42. 8.

free citizens which we find at this period. What can a civilized and sensitive man hope to do when flung into such a world? Only to be gentle, Menander seems to say: to remember that he is human, and nothing human is outside his range of sympathy. He can comfort his soul with the contemplation of 'sun and stars, water and clouds and fire', eternal beauties which remain while puny man strives and passes; he can possess his soul in patience and in kindliness, and remember always that here we have no abiding city.

That is the philosophic background of Menander's thought. But of course it is only the background. He is not a philosopher. He is a writer of comedy, a wit, an ingenious inventor, above all an observer of the oddities and humours of mankind. He is the maker, or at least the perfecter, of a new form of art.

The New Comedy is descended both from the Old Comedy of Aristophanes and from Euripidean tragedy. From Old Comedy it took its metres and scansion and the general style of its dialogue: also the idea of using an invented situation and imaginary characters, whereas Tragedy had been content to tell and re-tell the stories of the heroes as tradition had given them. It kept also much of the underlying atmosphere of the Old Comedy. It dealt with the present, not the past. It always contained a Kômos or Revel, always a Gamos, or Union of Lovers. Some elements in it, such as the

unescapable babies or twins, seem to go back to
the primitive fertility rites out of which the Old
Comedy developed. On the other hand, it rejected
many of the most characteristic features of the Old
Comedy. It rejected the phallic dress, the free
indecency of the language, the dances and the
songs; it rejected completely the political diatribes
and the criticism by name of public men. There
seems to have been no word in the New Comedy
of satire against the Macedonians, just as there was
never a word of flattery. The Chorus it treated in
a peculiar way. Apparently the public expected a
Chorus, but a poet like Menander did not con-
descend to write for it. Sometimes towards the
end of the First Act one of the characters observes that he sees a band of young men revelling
or dancing, or perhaps drunk, and proposes to get
out of their way.[1] The Chorus then enters and
performs. It is not mentioned again, but it performs in the intervals between the Acts.

In most other ways the New Comedy belongs
to the tradition of Tragedy, especially the tragedy
of Euripides. It took from there its elaborate plots;
for Euripides, though he kept religiously to the
traditional heroic legends, worked them out with
an ingenuity which amounted to invention. As his
biographer, Satyrus, expresses it, Euripides showed
invention in passionate scenes 'between husband
and wife, father and son, slave and master; in

---

[1] *Epitrep.* 33 ff.; *Perik.* 71 ff.

reversals of fortune; in ravished maidens and sup-
posititious children, and recognitions by means of
rings and necklaces. And out of these the New
Comedy is built up.'[1] Euripides had found these
elements already existing in the myths and rites
which lie at the back of Greek drama. The Year-
God is commonly a baby who grows up; he is
commonly a foundling, a child of unknown parents;
he is discovered or recognized as the child of a god.
But one can see that Euripides was always deepen-
ing and enriching his traditional motives by the
observation of real life. The saga gave him Ion as
the son of Apollo and the princess Creusa, a distinguished and satisfactory parentage. He made of
it a tragedy of lust and betrayal, the untroubled
and serene cruelty of the perfectly strong towards
the weak. Menander, going farther on the same
road, takes the decisive step of making his characters no longer gods or heroes or even princes,
but middle-class Athenian citizens of his own day.
His comedy belongs to what Diderot called *le
genre sérieux*; it was a comedy with thought and
with tears in it.

It is this affiliation, as Wilamowitz has seen, that
also explains the masks and stock characters of the
New Comedy. The tragic heroes by the end of
the fifth century, if not earlier, had their characters
known and fixed. Oedipus, Odysseus, Clytem-
nestra and the rest were known figures, as Crom-

---

[1] Ταῦτ' ἐστὶ τὰ συνέχοντα τὴν νεωτέραν κωμῳδίαν, Satyrus, col. vii.

well, Mary Queen of Scots, or Joan of Arc would
be now. They required no exposition or explanation, but each could proceed at once to act or speak
according to his traditional nature. They seem
also to have had recognizable masks, so that as soon
as Ajax or Orestes appeared, most of the audience
knew him. The New Comedy dropped the traditional heroic names. It used fictitious names and
characters; but it wanted still to use the technique
of the traditional subject. The audience was accustomed to it. It avoided the tedium of beginning
every play with scenes or even whole acts of mere
explanation and exposition. So it used typical
characters and typical masks. It is significant that
both in Greek and in Latin the word for mask is
also the word for character; and *Dramatis Personae*
means, strictly speaking, 'The Masks needed in
the Performance'. The cross elderly uncle had one
sort of mask, the indulgent elderly uncle another.
The Obstinate Man, the Flatterer, the Bragging
Soldier and the Modest Soldier were got up in such
a way that the audience could recognize each type,
whatever his name or adventures might be in the
particular play, almost as easily as the tragic
audience could recognize Ajax. Of course this
standardization of the masks tended to limit the
writer's invention. But it was not rigid. There are
ancient wall-paintings which represent a playwright criticizing a set of masks and having them
altered.

One often wonders that the masks of the New
Comedy, except for the conventional good looks
of the hero and heroine, were so far removed from
realism. To our taste they seem suited well enough
to an Aristophanic farce, but most odd in a refined
and perhaps touching Menandrian comedy. Part
of the explanation lies, no doubt, in the conditions
of the great open-air theatre and the absence of
opera glasses. Only very strong lines were visible;
and after all the audience had been accustomed to
masks from time immemorial. But I think that
perhaps there was deliberate intention in the avoidance of realism or life-likeness in the masks. We
must remember that it was forbidden to satirize
real persons on the stage. The rule was plain; but
supposing a mischievous playwright, without mentioning any names, put some offensive character
into a mask which closely resembled the face of
some real person, what then? It is just what Aristophanes had tried to do in the *Knights*, when he
wanted the mask-makers to make his Paphlagonian look like Cleon, and they prudently refused.[1] That such a thing should be possible would
make it suspected. If a comedian put a character
into any realistic mask, he might discover that the
Macedonian authorities thought it was too like the
Governor's cousin, and would come down on him

----

[1] Ar. *Knights*, 230-2 (cf. p. 41 above):

καὶ μὴ Δέδιθ'· οὐ γάρ ἐστιν ἐξηκασμένος,
ὑπὸ τοῦ Δέους γὰρ αὐτὸν οὐΔεὶς ἤθελεν
τῶν σκευοποιῶν εἰκάσαι.

with a fine or a sentence of exile. The only safe
course, when your characters were not meant for
pictures of real persons, was to put them in masks
which could not possibly be mistaken for any real
person.

Of course modifications would or could always
be made in the masks to suit the particular conception of the type-character. One cross uncle
was not necessarily the exact image of another.
And we must always be on guard against the mistake of imagining that the types were as limited
and rigid when the New Comedy was alive and
growing as they seemed to the grammarians who
classified them after it was dead. When any form
of art is dead, it is easy to catalogue its points and
fix its boundaries. When Dickens or Shakespeare
was alive, it probably seemed to contemporaries
that there was no limit to the creative imagination
of either: when their work is finished, we can go
through it and set down the limits within which it
moved. We must also realize that our remains are
too scanty to admit of a confident judgement, and
that the adaptations of Plautus, and even, I should
say, those of Terence, are lacking in that sensitiveness and flexibility which were characteristic of
Menander. Still, when all these allowances are
made, the impression left is that on the whole
Menander and his fellows, in spite of their great
originality and large productiveness, did mostly
operate by making different combinations of a

limited number of motives. A betrayed maiden,
a foundling and a recognition, a clever slave, a
severe father and an indulgent father, took them
a long way. Nevertheless, if one compares the
subjects treated by Menander with those of Aristophanes on the one hand and Euripides on the
other, the impression of diversity and abundance
of invention is overwhelming. Let us take, as an
indication, the names of a score or so of his lost
plays.

Several seem to deal with the fate of women
from captured cities: *The Woman from Andros*,
The Woman from Perinthus, *from Samos*, *from
Olynthus*, *from Thessaly*, *from Boeotia*, *from Leucas*: though doubtless the *Woman from Leucas* was
based on the old love-story of one who threw
herself into the sea from the Leucadian cliff, and
the *Woman from Thessaly* must have been given to
witchcraft. The *Man from Sicyon* was apparently
a sort of Tartarin, what the French call a Gascon,
in type, a talker and planner and promiser of great
things. The *Man from Carthage* we know was a
barbarian, talking broken Greek, pitifully searching the world for his two sons who had been captured in war, and eventually finding them. The
Perikeiromenê, or 'He clips her Hair', has been
discussed above; so has the *Misoumenos* or 'Hated'.

A great mass of plays deal with what the seventeenth century would have called 'humours'; the
quaint characteristics of human nature. The titles

are often impossible to translate owing to the differences in mere grammar between Greek and English: 'Ανατιθεμένη is perhaps *She Changes Her Mind*. But what is 'Ραπιזομένη? Perhaps *He Boxes Her Ears!* will do it, though possibly it is a theatrical or musical term and means 'Hissed Off'. *In Mourning for Himself*, Αὑτὸν Πενθῶν, suggests a play like Arnold Bennett's *Great Adventure*. *The Man who Punished Himself* did so, we happen to know, because his harsh discipline had made his son run away to the wars. *The Rustic, The Heiress, The Treasure, The Slanderer, The Flatterer, The Woman-hater, The Sea Captain, The Recruiting Officer, The Widow* seem fairly clear. So do *False!* (῎Απιστος), *Bad Temper,* and *Twice Deceived* (though in Greek the participle is active); we know something of the last from a brilliant scene in Plautus's *Bacchides*, where the slave Chrysalus, who has just cheated his master's father out of 200 Philippi, been found out and compelled to restore the money, is then required to deceive the old man again and get it back![1] *The Imbrians* or *Gone to Imbros* was supposed to refer to the fact that that island was the nearest place in which to escape extradition for debt and small offences: there is an old English farce with the title *A Bolt to Boulogne*. A new fragment, however, throws doubt on this.[2] *Thais* and *Phanion* are named from their

---

[1] Plaut. *Bacch.* IV. v–viii, ll. 760 sqq.
[2] *P. Oxyrh.* x. 1235.

heroines, and the names are not the names of respectable citizens. Other plays are almost impossible to translate: Κωνειαζόμεναι describing women who for some reason threaten to drink hemlock; Συναριστῶσαι or *Ladies Lunching together*; Συνερῶσα, which seems to mean *She Also Loved Him*; Συνέφηβοι, *Both Were Young*; Πρόγαμοι or Προγάμια, *Before the Marriage*. There seems an immense variety, and of course I have taken only a few out of the many titles preserved. Tradition says that Menander was a friend, and perhaps a follower, of Epicurus. If so, we need not be surprised to find a group of plays dealing with superstition: *The Superstitious Man, Trophônius*—a reference to the famous and somewhat ridiculous oracle in Boeotia—*The Begging Priest, Inspired,* and *The Priestess*. In *The Apparition* the plot presents us with a widower who has married again: his new wife has a grown-up daughter whose existence she has concealed, but from whom she cannot bear to be parted. She constructs a shrine in her house, with a curtain in front and a secret exit, and here her daughter visits her. Her step-son, who is surprised at his step-mother's extreme piety, catches sight in the shrine of a mysterious figure, which is explained by those interested as being a divine apparition. One sees the start for a comedy of mystification.

The titles form, of course, a slender foundation on which to rest any very definite belief about the

qualities of the plays; but the impression which
they make is greatly strengthened by what little
we know of the plots. We have, for example, on
a fragmentary papyrus part of an account of the
plot of *The Priestess*.[1] A man's wife or mistress
had left him long ago—perhaps for religious
reasons—and become a priestess. He does not
know what she did with their son, and the Priestess
is unapproachable. She is, however, an adept at
exorcisms; so the man's confidential slave pretends
to be possessed by a demon, has a fit on the temple
steps, and is taken in by the Priestess for treatment.
He finds out that the boy is being reared as their
own by some people called *X*, and tells the father,
who goes at once to claim his son. But it so happens
that the *X*'s have also a son of their own, and by
mistake the excited old gentleman lights on him
and claims to be his father by telling a story which
is obviously absurd. The boy decides that the old
gentleman is mad, and tells his foster-brother;
who consequently, when his father, now better
informed, approaches him on the same subject,
humours him as a lunatic. I omit some minor
complications; but even thus one sees what an
immense advance in the mechanism of plot-
construction and entanglement has been made
since the fifth century.

In the *Woman of Samos*, again, we can make out
from the 340 lines now extant the outlines of a

[1] *Pap. Oxyrh.* x. 1235.

lively and intricate, though doubtless highly artificial plot.

The characters belong to two families. One
consists of Demeas, a rich citizen, his adopted son
Moschio, and his concubine Chrysis, the 'Samian
Woman', free-born but enslaved through war, who
has just lost her first child. There are also a household slave Parmeno, a Nurse and a comic Cook.
Next door lives Nicêratus, poor but proud, with
his portionless daughter, Plangon. Moschio and
Plangon love each other, but both fathers have forbidden the marriage. Meantime the young people,
left alone, have come together secretly, and,
while the fathers are away on a voyage, Plangon
has a baby, which has to be concealed, and which
Chrysis, mourning for her dead child, is persuaded
to take and rear as her own. The two fathers
return; something has happened—there is here a
gap in the papyrus—to change their minds, and
they have agreed to the marriage of Moschio
and Plangon. Demeas is pleased with the baby
which Chrysis shows him, and the wedding feast
is ordered, when suddenly things begin to go
wrong. Demeas overhears the nurse speaking of
the baby as if it was Moschio's child. Much upset,
he questions the slave Parmeno, whose frightened
prevarications convince him of the worst. Moschio,
whom he loved as a son, has seduced Chrysis,
whom he trusted as a wife! His world crumbles
about his ears, and he jumps to the conclusion that

it is all the fault of Chrysis! Sweeping aside the
Cook, who has come to talk at length about the
wedding breakfast, he dashes into the house, and
drives Chrysis and the baby out into the street.
Chrysis herself, Parmeno, and even the Cook try
to get some explanation from the furious and
broken-hearted old man; but he will not publish
his own dishonour, and gives none. At this moment
Nicêratus appears on the scene, tries in vain to
check his friend's madness, and at last, defying
him, takes the weeping Chrysis into his own house.

At the opening of the next act, Moschio, who
knows nothing of what has happened, has made
up his mind to go to his adopted father, confess
his fault and humbly beg forgiveness. Demeas is
in the blackest mood and difficult to approach,
but, as the confession proceeds, cheers up in a surprising way, forgives and almost congratulates the
sinner, and is left beaming. Chrysis and Moschio
were not false to him after all. His honour is
saved! Nothing is wrong—except for this little
indiscretion of Moschio and Plangon, naughty
young things! He meets Nicêratus, and tells him
the facts with laughter and self-congratulations.
'Congratulations!' roars the other old gentleman,
'when my daughter has disgraced my name for
ever!' He will punish the girl and put to death
the bastard. Rushing in to do so he finds Chrysis,
who valiantly claims the baby as hers, makes
Plangon and her mother refuse to admit anything,

and, in a scene exactly parallel to that in the last act, is driven out by her former protector and protected by her former persecutor. The two old men are again left together, with their roles reversed. Demeas first fights, then reproaches, then comforts his proud and choleric old friend, and at last formally asks, on behalf of Moschio, for the hand of Plangon in marriage.

All is ending happily, when a new complication occurs. Moschio, who had been surprised at the beaming satisfaction with which Demeas had accepted his confession of sin, has learnt meantime the explanation and is deeply hurt. How could his father have dreamed that he would be capable of such villainy? He cannot forgive him. He will not be reconciled. He will leave the country. He will go and enlist . . . at least he would if it was not for Plangon!

At this tantalizing point the papyrus breaks off. One may conjecture that poor Demeas finds he has to apologize not only to his adopted son but to a much more formidable and more deeply wronged person, the Samian Woman. Chrysis has had enough of the two half-lunatic old men; they have both driven her out with the child. 'Good!' she may say, 'the child has been given her; she will take it and not come back!' . . . How the peace is made we cannot say, but no doubt in the end the two old gentlemen are found kneeling for pardon to their respective families, the citizenship of

Chrysis is somehow discovered or re-established, and the play ends with a double marriage, Demeas and Chrysis, Moschio and Plangon.

Tragedy, to use the old Roman division, dealt with *Res Sacra*; the Comedy of Aristophanes dealt with *Res Publica*; that of Menander was occupied with *Res Privata*, a region in which the emotions and changes of fortune may be smaller in extent, but are infinitely more various.

No less marked than the development of plot is the development of technique in points of detail. The number of actors is no longer limited to three. The metres are those of Comedy, though the musical and lyrical element is entirely absent. It is notable that Menander is more concerned with metrical euphony and with a skilful ordering of the words in the sentence than his contemporaries. He avoids, for example, the so-called 'pause after a dactyl', and seldom admits inversions of order for merely metrical reasons. The language though strikingly natural is never slangy or vulgar.[1] He avoids scrupulously forms of words that were not really colloquial, such as Datives in -οισι or -αισι, while he elides freely the verbal termination -αι, which at this time was pronounced like ε. In sum one may say that while he has built up a most

[1] The presence of an obscene phrase in one papyrus fragment has been taken as evidence that the fragment is not the work of Menander. A passage in *Perik.* 234, where a slave makes a coarse joke to a Hetaira, who is offended by it, is an exception which proves the rule.

scrupulous and delicate style of his own, he is wonderfully free from the influence of professional rhetoric. Then there are great variety and flexibility in the composition. People enter 'talking off stage': or conversing with each other; they enter in the middle of a sentence or a line. The soliloquies, which are not uncommon, are real soliloquies, in which embarrassed persons try to get things clear by talking to themselves: they are not, except in the Prologues, mere devices for telling a story. Sometimes the soliloquies are overheard: a device which is suitable enough when the speaker has really been talking to himself aloud, though very bad when the soliloquy is only the playwright's artifice for revealing a character's unspoken thoughts. Conversations are overheard and interrupted: there are misunderstandings which lead to results; there are motives of action based deliberately on odd or over-subtle points of psychology. Thus Moschio, when all his wishes are granted, is nevertheless so hurt at having been previously misunderstood, that he determines not indeed to enlist but to pretend that he intends to enlist, so that his father may be sorry and beg him to stay. And, though the play there breaks off, we may hazard a guess that the father is either too stupid or too clever, or too full of self-reproach to do what he is expected to do. Such refinements are more in the style of the Parisian stage in the nineteenth century than that of classical Athens.

At times it would seem that a complication is invented chiefly for the sake of the psychology. It gives the opportunity for some one to act not in the ordinary way but in some strange way that illustrates the oddity of human nature. In *The Samian Woman*, when the baby, with the diabolical ingenuity that distinguishes Menander's babies, contrives to make Demeas believe that it is the child of the Samian Woman and his adopted son, the deceived man breaks out into a fury of rage and curses, but instantly checks himself. 'Why are you shouting? Fool, why are you shouting? Control yourself. Be patient. . . . It is not Moschio's fault. He did not mean it. He would never want to wrong me. He has always been good to me and to every one. She must have taken him in a weak moment. Fascinated the boy as she fascinated me . . . who am much older and ought to be wiser. She is a Helen! A siren! A harlot!'[1] The unnatural gentleness of his first reaction leads to the violent explosion of his next.

Then the method of exposition, if not altogether new—for both Comedy and Tragedy had not merely their prologues but their scenes with two characters in conversation indirectly explaining the situation of the play[2]—is nevertheless far more varied and ingenious than any in the fifth century

---

[1] *Samia*, 111–33.

[2] Two servants in the *Medea* and the *Knights*: Dionysus and Xanthias in the *Frogs*, Antigone and Ismene in the *Antigone*, and so on.

had tried to be. Menander contrives to amuse you
in a dozen different ways while he makes his explanation. Let us take the scene which gives its
name to the *Epitrepontes*, the scene of the Arbitration. What is needed for the plot is to explain that
a certain exposed baby has been reared, and will
prove to be the child of Charisius. But the way
the story is told is this.[1]

Enter two slaves, a charcoal-burner and a shepherd, quarrelling, followed by a woman with a
baby. 'You are cheating.' 'No, it's you.' 'Oh,
why did I give him anything?' 'Will you agree
to an arbitration?' 'Yes; where shall we find
the arbitrator?' 'Any one will do. Try this old
gentleman.'

The old gentleman, Smicrines, is just returning
in an angry temper from the house of his son-in-
law, Charisius.

THE CHARCOAL-BURNER. Please, Sir, could you spend
a few minutes on us?

OLD GENTLEMAN. On you? Why?

CHARC. We are having a dispute.

O.G. What is that to me?

CHARC. We are looking for an arbitrator. If there is
nothing to prevent you, you might settle . . .

O.G. Bless my soul! Peasants in goatskins walking
about and litigating as they go!

The Charcoal-burner pleads with him, and
pleads so eloquently that the Shepherd is alarmed.

---

[1] Ἐπιτρέποντες, ll. 1–177.

SHEPHERD. How he does talk! Oh, why did I ever give him anything?

O.G. You will abide by my decision?

CHARC. Yes, whatever it is.

O.G. All right, I will hear the case. . . . You begin, Shepherd, as you have not spoken yet.

Every line so far is slightly unexpected and therefore amusing. You cannot help wanting to hear what comes next.

The Shepherd begins:

About a month ago I was watching my sheep alone on some wooded ground, when I found a baby lying on the grass with a necklace and some ornaments.

CHARC. (*interrupting*). That is what it's all about.

SHEP. (*turning on him*). He says you are not to speak!

O.G. If you interrupt I will hit you with my stick.

SHEP. Quite right too. (*The Charcoal-burner subsides.*)

SHEP. (*continuing*). I brought the baby home. Then at night I thought it over. How was I to bring up a child? Next day this charcoal-burner met me and I told him what had happened, and he begged me to give him the child. 'For God's sake', he said, 'let me have it, and I will bless you. My wife has had a baby, and it has died.' .

O.G. (*to Charcoal-burner*). Did you ask him for it?

CHARC. I did.

SHEP. He spent the whole day beseeching me. When I gave it to him he kissed my hands.

O.G. Did you kiss his hands?

CHARC. I did.

SHEP. So he went off. Then next day suddenly he came back with his wife and demanded the ornaments and things—not that they are of any value—which had been exposed with the child. Now, obviously, they have nothing to do with the case. He asked for the baby and I gave him the baby. What I found belongs to me, and he ought to be grateful that I gave him part of it. That is all I have to say. (*A pause.*)

CHARC. Has he quite finished?

O.G. Yes. Didn't you hear him say so?

CHARC. Very good. Then I answer. His account is perfectly correct. He found the child. I begged him to give me the child. All quite true. Then I heard from one of his fellow-shepherds that he had found some trinkets with the child. Those trinkets are the child's property, and here is the child claiming them. (Bring him forward, wife!) They are his, not yours; and I, as his guardian and protector, demand them on his behalf. His whole fortune in life may depend on those trinkets. They may enable us to identify his parents, like Neleus or Pelias in the tragedies.—Now please decide.

O.G. All that was exposed with the child belongs to the child. That is my decision.

SHEP. Very good; but in that case whom does the child belong to?

O.G. Not to you who tried to rob it. I award the child to this Charcoal-burner who has tried to protect it.

CHARC. God bless you!

SHEP. A monstrous judgement. Good Lord, I found everything, and it is all taken from me! . . . Have I got to give the things up?

O.G. Certainly.

SHEP. Monstrous! Plague take me if it isn't!

CHARC. Be quick.

SHEP. Heracles, what treatment!

CHARC. Open your bag and let us see the things. . . . Please don't go yet; wait, Sir, till he hands them over

SHEP. (*handing the things slowly over*). Why did I ever trust this man to arbitrate?

O.G. Hand them over, rascal.

SHEP. I call it disgraceful.

O.G. Have you got them all? Then good-bye!

One might think the scene was now exhausted of all its dramatic points; but not at all. The Shepherd goes off grumbling. The Charcoal-burner sits down with his wife to look through the trinkets one by one. While they are doing so, Onesimus, the slave of Charisius, happens to come out of the house, and naturally looks to see what the pair are doing.

'A seal with a cock on it', proceeds the Charcoal-burner. 'A transparent stone. An axe-head. A signet ring with the stone set in gold, the rest of it iron; the figure of a goat or a bull, I can't see which. Name of the carver Cleostratus. . . .'

ONESIMUS. Let's have a look!

CHARC. Hullo, who are you?

ON. That's it!

CHARC. What's it?

ON. The ring.

CHARC. What about it?

ON. It's the ring my master lost.

There we may stop. Of course, by strict standards the scene is an artificial one, though the incidents are not impossible nor outside the range of common life. But the treatment shows a light touch and a variety of incident which mark a complete change from the style of the fifth century. Every line has a certain unobtrusive wit, the quality that was called in antiquity 'Attic salt', and the situation is made to yield its full harvest of amusement.

If this scene is leisurely in movement, let us take another from the same play to show how swift Menander can be, when he wishes, with his big emotional effects.

A harp-player named Habrotonon,[1] moved partly by pity, partly by a wish to get her freedom, pretends that the child is hers. This gives her a hold over Charisius. Meantime she is looking for the real mother. She remembers seeing a girl with torn clothes, crying bitterly at the feast of the Tauropolia, and is sure that there she has a clue. Charisius's young wife, Pamphile, who is distracted between the unkindness of her husband and the fury with which her father takes her part against him, comes out of her house just as Habrotonon with the baby comes out of the next house.

PAM. (*to herself*). My eyes are sore with crying.

HAB. (*to the baby*). Poor thing! Did it keep whining? What did it want, then?

PAM. (*to herself*). Will no god take pity on me?

HAB. Dear baby, when will you find your mother?— But who is this?

PAM. (*to herself*). Well, I will go back to my father.

HAB. (*staring at her*). Madam, wait one moment!

PAM. Did you speak to me?

HAB. Yes. Oh, look at me! Do you know me?—

---

[1] 'Επιτρέποντες, 432–51.

This is the girl I saw. . . . (*impulsively*) Oh, my dear, I am so glad.

PAM. (*frightened*). Who are you?

HAB. Give me your hand. Tell me, dear, last year you went, didn't you, to the Tauropolia . . .

PAM. (*noticing the baby*). Woman, where did you get that child?

HAB. Poor darling, do you see something you know, round its neck? . . . (*Drawing back*) Oh, madam, don't be frightened of me.

PAM. It is not your own child?

HAB. I have pretended it was. Not that I meant to cheat the real mother. I only wanted to find her. . . . And now you are found! You are the girl I saw that night.

PAM. (*Only one thought in her mind*) Who was the man?

HAB. Charisius.

PAM. Oh joy! . . . Do you know it? Are you sure?

A scene could hardly be more rapid, and every word tells.

The literary fate of Menander has been curious. He was apparently a little too subtle, too refined, too averse from rhetoric, or possibly too new and original, for the popular taste of his own day. With over a hundred plays he only obtained the first prize eight times. He was obviously not a best-seller. But his fame was immense, and he was recognized soon after his death as the incontestable chief of the writers of the New Comedy. Almost alone in his age he ranked as a classic; and the Atticist grammarians of Roman times have to

labour the point that Menander, however illus-
trious, did not really write the perfect Attic of
Plato or old Aristophanes.

More than this, the style of drama which he
brought to perfection proceeded immediately to
dominate the ancient stage. The Hellenistic theatre
knew no other form of comedy: the Roman theatre
lived entirely on translations and adaptations of
Menander and his school, Philêmon, Diphilus,
Posidippus, and the rest. He was read and praised
by Cicero and Quintilian; by Plutarch, Lucian,
Alciphron, Aelian; he is quoted in anthologies,
and his apophthegms were made up into anthologies of their own. But in modern times, when the
Renaissance scholars proceeded to look for his
plays, it was found that they had all perished.
They were only represented by the Roman adaptations of Plautus and Terence, the former much
rougher, coarser, and more boisterous in form,
the latter showing much delicacy of style, but
somewhat flattened and enfeebled.

Yet through these inferior intermediaries Menander conquered the modern stage. There is not
much of him in Shakespeare except the *Comedy of
Errors*. But Molière with *L'Avare* and *Le Misan-
thrope*, with *Les Femmes savantes* and above all
Les Fourberies de Scapin, comes straight out of the
Menander tradition. So does Beaumarchais with
his *Figaro* and his *Don César de Bazan*. And the
style of both has the Menandrian polish. The

great Danish comedian Holberg confessedly went back to Plautus for some of his plays, and adopted Menandrian formulae for others. In England there is a touch of him in Ben Jonson. There are whole blocks of him in Congreve, Farquhar, and Vanbrugh—the same dissipated young men, the same clever and knavish servants, the same deceiving of parents and guardians, the same verbal courtliness and wit, the same elaboration of the story. Sheridan, though more of a gentleman than the Restoration Dramatists, belongs to the same school, and has built Sir Anthony Absolute and the Captain, Charles Surface and Joseph Surface, quite on the Menandrian model. Of course these writers only knew Plautus and Terence, and were doubtless content with their models. They had little of Menander's philosophic spirit, nothing of his interest in distressed women; nothing of his inexhaustible human sympathies and profound tenderness of heart. But, directly or indirectly, no one who writes polite comedy can avoid the influence of Menander.

It is a curious thing, this power of world-wide and almost inexhaustible influence. A price has to be paid for it, and a heavy price. A writer cannot be so popular unless he is, I will not say, vulgar himself, but at least capable of being read with pleasure by vulgar people. All great writers and thinkers need interpreters: otherwise the difference between them and the average lazy public is too great. And it is likely enough that Menander has gained in influence rather than lost through his dependence on his Roman imitators. They had left out his delicacy of thought, his reflectiveness, and much of his beauty of style, but they kept the good broad lines that were easy for every one to understand.

Thus the interpreters and inheritors were provided. But, to justify such a long life for Menander's influence, there must have been something to interpret, some inheritance precious enough to compel the interest of successive generations. And I think we can see what there was. There go to the greatest imaginative work normally two qualities: intensity of experience and the gift of transmuting intensity into beauty. Menander had both. Gibbon speaks somewhere of the intense suffering which is caused when a refined and sensitive population is put under the control of brutal and uneducated conquerors, or, what comes to much the same thing, exposed to the brutal play of chance. He was thinking of the highly civilized Byzantines put at the mercy of the Turks: we may think of the many sensitive natures who were broken or driven mad by the strain of service in the late war. Menander belonged to just such a refined and sensitive generation—the most civilized known to the world before that date, and perhaps for two thousand years after it—flung suddenly into a brutal and violently changing world. He interpreted its experience in his own characteristic way: not by a great spiritual defiance, like the Stoic or Cynic; not by flight from the world, like the Epicurean; but by humour, by patience, by a curious and searching sympathy with his fellow mortals, in their wrigglings as well as their firm stands; and by a singular power of expressing their thoughts and their strange ways in language so exact and simple and satisfying that the laughter in it seldom hurts, and the pain is suffused with beauty.

CHRONOLOGICAL TABLE OF
ARISTOPHANES' PLAYS

450–444? Aristophanes, son of Philippos of Kudathenaion, born.

432 Peloponnesian War declared.

430 Plague of Athens.

429 Death of Pericles.

427 *Daitalês*; the two sons. Against the new city culture. (*Cl.* 529.) Second Prize.
Reduction of Mitylênê: Cleon's policy of 'mass terror'. (Thuc. iii. 36 ff.)

426 Dionysia: the *Babylonians*; attack on all Athenian authorities, especially Cleon. Allied Cities as slaves on a treadmill. Aristophanes prosecuted and 'almost killed' by Cleon. (*Ach.* 377 ff.)

425 Lenaea: the *Acharnians* (First Prize: Cratînus, Χειμαζόμενοι, 2nd; Eupolis, Νουμήνιαι, 3rd). Dicaiopolis makes peace alone; Lamachus represents war-party.
August: Triumph of Cleon at Pylos.

424 Lenaea: the *Knights* (First Prize: Cratînus, *Satyri*, 2nd; Aristomenes, *Hylophori*, 3rd). Attack on Cleon: regeneration of Athens. Quarrel with Eupolis: *Cl.* 553 ff. and Eupolis, *Baptae*.

423 Lenaea? the *Holkades*, against Cleon's satellites: *Wasps*, 1038. (Cf. Massacre of Skiônê in 421.)
Dionysia: the *Clouds*, on the new philosophic movement, typified in Socrates (3rd: beaten by Cratînus, Πυτίνη, *The Bottle*, 1st, and Ameipsias, *Konnos*, 2nd—Why?). Changes in the second edition show more definite polemic against Socrates. *Cl.* 521 ff.

422 Lenaea: the *Wasps* (2nd: 1st, 'Philônides', *Proagon*; 3rd, Leucon, *Ambassadors*). Attack on savage Jury Courts and 'Philocleon'. Hero, 'Bdelycleon'. Dionysia? the *Georgoi*, similar to the *Peace*. Autumn: Deaths of Brasidas and Cleon.

421 Dionysia. The *Peace* (2nd: 1st, Eupolis, *Kolakes*, flatterers of the rich Callias, non-political; 3rd, Leucon, *Phratores*). Idyllic and Panhellenic. Trygaios on beetle.
  Peace of Nicias.
  Skiônê captured: all adult males massacred according to decree carried by Cleon, executed after his death.

? *Gêras* or 'Old Age'. Rejuvenation.

416 Winter: massacre of Melos.

415 Eupolis, *Baptae*, against Alcibiades.
  May: Mutilation of the Hermae.
  July: Start of Expedition to conquer Sicily and the West. Recall and flight of Alcibiades.

414 Lenaea: *Amphiarâus*. Man and Wife rejuvenated at Amphiarâus's temple at Orôpus.
  Dionysia: the *Birds* (2nd: 1st, Ameipsias, *Komastai*; 3rd, Phrynichus, *Monotropos* (Solitary)). Founding of the Cloud-City.

413 Disastrous end of Sicilian Expedition. Sparta declares war.

411 Lenaea: (February?) the *Lysistrata*, General Strike of Women to enforce Peace.
  March. Revolution: Oligarchy of the Four Hundred.
  July: Rule of the Five Thousand. Recall of Alcibiades.

410 Lenaea(?): the *Thesmophoriazûsae*. Euripides and the Athenian Women.

408 First *Plutus*, not preserved.—Also, date unknown, a second *Thesmophoriazûsae?*

The *Triphalês*, probably on Alcibiades.

[Uncertain date, *Lemniai* (on legend of the Lemnian Women and the Argonauts; perhaps reference to worship of Bendis, the Thracian Goddess); *Gerytades* (embassy of various artists to Hades for advice from the great masters); *Phoenissae* (parody of Euripides' tragedy?).]

406 Victory of Arginûsae.

Death of Euripides, and, later, of Sophocles.

405 Lenaea: the *Frogs* (1st: 2nd, Phrynichus, *Muses*; 3rd, Plato, *Cleophon*). Contest of Aeschylus and Euripides in Hades for the Throne of Poetry. Some time after this *Dramata* or *Niobos*, possibly representing the action brought against Sophocles by his son Iophon?

404 June: Fall of Athens. Destruction of the Long Walls. The Thirty Tyrants.

403 Defeat of the Thirty. Return of the Demos.

399 Condemnation and death of Socrates.

395 League of Athens, Thebes, Corinth, Thessaly, Argos. Long Walls rebuilt.

392? The *Ecclesiazûsae*. Social revolution and rule of women, on lines of Plato's *Republic* (parodied).

388 *Plutus*, healing of the blind God. Beginning of transition to Middle or New Comedy. (Five poets competing, by new law.)

Later: the *Kôkalus* (the Daedalus story, with romantic plot, like Menander), and *Aiolosikon* (Aeolus as Cook?) a burlesque in style of Middle Comedy burlesques, handed over to his son Arârôs.

INDEX

PRINTED IN GREAT BRITAIN AT THE UNIVERSITY PRESS, OXFORD
BY VIVIAN RIDLER, PRINTER TO THE UNIVERSITY